DINNER WITH THE FAMILY

A Play in Three Acts

by
JEAN ANOUILH

Translated by
EDWARD OWEN MARSH

LONDON
SAMUEL FRENCH LIMITED

Copyright © 1958 by Jean Anouilh and Edward Owen Marsh
All Rights Reserved

DINNER WITH THE FAMILY is fully protected under the copyright laws of the British Commonwealth, including Canada, the United States of America, and all other countries of the Copyright Union. All rights, including professional and amateur stage productions, recitation, lecturing, public reading, motion picture, radio broadcasting, television and the rights of translation into foreign languages are strictly reserved.

ISBN 978-0573-01106-1

concordtheatricals.co.uk

concordtheatricals.com

FOR AMATEUR PRODUCTION ENQUIRIES

UNITED KINGDOM AND WORLD EXCLUDING NORTH AMERICA

licensing@concordtheatricals.co.uk

020-7054-7200

Each title is subject to availability from Samuel French, depending upon country of performance.

CAUTION: Professional and amateur producers are hereby warned that DINNER WITH THE FAMILY is subject to a licensing fee. Publication of this play does not imply availability for performance. Both amateurs and professionals considering a production are strongly advised to apply to the appropriate agent before starting rehearsals, advertising, or booking a theatre. A licensing fee must be paid whether the title is presented for charity or gain and whether or not admission is charged.

The Professional Rights in this play are controlled by Agence MCR, 11, rue Le Regrattier 75004 Paris.

No one shall make any changes in this title for the purpose of production. No part of this book may be reproduced, stored in a retrieval system, or transmitted in any form, by any means, now known or yet to be invented, including mechanical, electronic, photocopying, recording, videotaping, or otherwise, without the prior written permission of the publisher. No one shall upload this title, or part of this title, to any social media websites.

The right of Jean Anouilh and Edward Owen Marsh to be identified as authors of this work has been asserted in accordance with Section 77 of the Copyright, Designs and Patents Act 1988.

DINNER WITH THE FAMILY

Produced at the New Theatre, London, on the 10th December 1957 with the following cast of characters—

(in the order of their appearance)

PROPRIETRESS	*Gwen Nelson*
GEORGES DELACHAUME, a young man	*John Justin*
EMILE, the butler	*Richard Dare*
DELMONTE, an actor	*Alan MacNaughton*
MME DE MONTRACHET, an actress	*Lally Bowers*
BARBARA, Jacques' wife; Georges' mistress	*Delena Kidd*
JACQUES, Georges' friend	*Ian Hendry*
M. DELACHAUME, Georges' father	*Edward Harvey*
ESME, a maid	*Jocelyne Page*
MME DELACHAUME, Georges' mother	*Gabrielle Hamilton*
ISABELLE, a young girl	*Jill Bennett*
THE DOCTOR	*Michael Bilton*

Directed by FRANK HAUSER
Settings by PAUL MAYO

SYNOPSIS OF SCENES

ACT I

The drawing-room of a large house in Senlis, some twenty-five miles from Paris. Early evening in Summer.

ACT II

SCENE 1 The linen-room in Christine's house in Paris. Five minutes later.
SCENE 2 The drawing-room at Senlis. About an hour later.

ACT III

The drawing-room at Senlis. An hour or so later.
Time—the present

DINNER WITH THE FAMILY

ACT I

SCENE—*The drawing-room of a large house in Senlis, some twenty-five miles from Paris. Early evening in Summer.*

It is a rococo room with double doors up LC *leading to the entrance hall and stairs, and there are french windows up* RC. *There is a secret door down* R, *concealed by a what-not affixed to it. A baby grand piano stands down* L *with a stool and folding screen above it. Small armchairs stand* LC *and up* C *and there is a sofa* RC, *a small chair down* R *and small tables above the secret door* R, *and* R *and* L *of the double doors. There is a telephone on the table above the doors. At night the room is lit by wall-brackets down* L *and up* C, *a standard lamp* R *and a table-lamp beside the telephone. The hall is furnished with two tables, a cabinet gramophone, a small chair, and a potted fern on a pedestal.*

(*See the Ground Plan of the Scene*)

When the CURTAIN *rises, the room is empty, but the double doors are open and the* PROPRIETRESS *and* GEORGES DELACHAUME *can be seen in the hall. The* PROPRIETRESS *is reading from a large-size inventory.*

PROPRIETRESS (*reading*) "One mahogany dumb-waiter—"
GEORGES. "One mahogany dumb-waiter."
PROPRIETRESS. "—and four copper flower-pots chased and ornamented." (*She comes into the room*)
GEORGES (*in tired repetition*) "Four ornamented flower-pots." Yes—they're there—they would be.
PROPRIETRESS. I beg your pardon?
GEORGES (*coming into the room*) I was saying how lovely they are.
PROPRIETRESS. I should think so. They were a wedding present.
GEORGES (*defeated by this argument*) Oh! Of course.
PROPRIETRESS. That's finished the dining-room. Now we come to the large drawing-room. We'll begin with the walls again. Let me see. (*She reads*) "Walls covered in figured silk with a delicate design of trees, flowers and birds."

(GEORGES *crosses to the wall down* L *and examines the wallpaper*)

GEORGES. I'm sorry. Do you mind if I stop you there? I can't see any birds.
PROPRIETRESS. Can't you? Really?
GEORGES. No. I'm not trying to be awkward. There just aren't any birds. (*He crosses to the Proprietress*) Let me see your inventory. (*He reads*) "Walls covered in figured silk, with a delicate design of trees, flowers *and birds.*" We are in the drawing-room, I suppose?

PROPRIETRESS. Of course! I know my own house, I hope.
GEORGES. Trees, yes—at a pinch you could even guess at the flowers, but, with the best will in the world, I can't see a bird. Look for yourself.

(*The* PROPRIETRESS *moves to the wall* R *of the doors and puts some effort into searching for the birds.* GEORGES *follows*)

PROPRIETRESS. I'm not wearing my spectacles, you see.
GEORGES. The day I leave this house I don't want to find I'm legally bound to pay for a flock of imaginary birds. (*He wanders* L, *examining the room*)
PROPRIETRESS (*moving* C; *bewildered*) I've had these inventories a long, long time just as they are. No-one's ever questioned them before. It was a very competent man indeed who did them for me.
GEORGES. Perhaps the birds were taken away by the previous tenant.
PROPRIETRESS (*attempting a wan smile*) From a wall pattern?
GEORGES. There's no limit now-a-days to what people steal. Anyway, there's no disputing it, there isn't a trace of a bird on the whole wall. Not a feather.

(*The* PROPRIETRESS *moves to the armchair up* C, *puts the inventory on it, then examines the wall*)

PROPRIETRESS (*who has not yet lost all hope*) This little design here? Don't you think . . .?

(GEORGES *crosses to the Proprietress*)

Here—the head—there, the tail?
GEORGES. A bird with a beak growing out of its stomach?
PROPRIETRESS. What shall we do, then?
GEORGES. I can only see one thing to do: scrap the inventory. (*He moves to the sofa and sits*)
PROPRIETRESS (*moving* C) You think that's funny? Anyone can see you're young. If you were my age you'd have something else to think about, a few worries to spoil the fun you seem to get out of life.
GEORGES (*rising and moving to the window; with a sudden sad crease in his lips*) Oh, worry's got a taste for young flesh, too.
PROPRIETRESS (*crossing to Georges*) Listen! I'll leave just the "trees and flowers". Let's forget the birds, shall we?
GEORGES. Thank you. Now, have we many more rooms to see?
PROPRIETRESS (*picking up the inventory and moving* C) How impatient you are. We've only done the dining-room and the hall, so far; there are still the two drawing-rooms and seven rooms upstairs.
GEORGES (*looking at his watch*) It's taken us thirty-five minutes

to do these two rooms. (*He crosses to the Proprietress and takes the inventory*) There are nine more. That makes about—three hours if we work steadily through the lot.
PROPRIETRESS (*very proudly*) Yes. This inventory runs to ninety-two pages. (*She takes the inventory from him*)
GEORGES. Does it really? I'm afraid I'm expecting some people by the seven-ten train and it's now two minutes to seven. So I have a total of twelve minutes at your disposal. Which room shall we do?
PROPRIETRESS (*hopping with emotion*) Twelve minutes! Why, it's ridiculous.
GEORGES. Quite!
PROPRIETRESS. But you can't blame me, can you, when you come wanting the house all in five minutes?

(GEORGES *wanders to the piano*)

(*She follows Georges*) You took it as from the first of the month, I know, but you didn't move in. I couldn't check the inventory without you. And now you drop in on me without warning, at a meal time, and everything's got to be done in a flash. I think I'm being very accommodating in allowing you to move in at all at this time of day. You know it's not usual.
GEORGES (*sitting at the piano*) My plans changed suddenly. I must have the house this evening. (*He plays a few bars*)
PROPRIETRESS. Well, if you must, you must, but an inventory is an inventory, remember. (*She tries a bold stroke*) Come, we'll go through it quickly. We won't look at the servants' rooms today. You see, I'm doing my best to meet you. Let me see (*She reads*) ". . . with trees and flowers . . ." (*She moves up* C) "At the windows, two large red damask curtains and holders made of the same metal." (*She moves* C)
GEORGES. The same metal? What metal?
PROPRIETRESS. How do you mean—"what metal"?
GEORGES. I think you'd better read that item again. Then you'll see for yourself.
PROPRIETRESS (*reading*) ". . . two large red damask curtains and holders made of the same metal." (*She repeats*) ". . . of the same metal." (*She thinks for a moment*) Yes, there must be a mistake, or a line missed out. He was a very competent man, you know, but of course, he was rather old.
GEORGES (*rising and moving to the Proprietress*) Far too old. It's crawling with mistakes—and you want me to sign that? I'm ready to believe in your good faith, but there is a limit. "Curtains and holders of the same metal." There's no mention of any metal. What if, the day I leave, you come down on me for a set of gold holders for your damask curtains?
PROPRIETRESS. Gold holders? Oh, no, you're joking.
GEORGES. You would be well within your rights. I know what

a signature can involve. I'm not prepared to spend any more time on this fantastic inventory. You can tell the aged and competent gentleman responsible for it . . .

PROPRIETRESS. He's dead.

GEORGES. Then you mustn't disturb him. (*He takes the inventory and crosses to the piano*) Give me the inventory. I'll sign it. This is to stop you worrying—people always exaggerate their worries at your age. That's their mistake. You can always smooth out life's little difficulties, you know, somehow. At least for one evening. With a little imagination a man can live his whole life in the space of an evening. (*He signs the inventory*) "Read and approved. Georges Delachaume." (*He moves to the Proprietress and hands her the inventory*) There! Now, it will all seem much simpler. (*He looks at his watch*) In eleven minutes' time everything in your house must be mine, including the invisible birds on the figured silk and the curtain holders made of the same metal.

PROPRIETRESS (*a little frightened by this flow of words*) Yours— yours? But we must understand one another, please, M. Delachaume—I mean—I know you've taken it furnished for the month, but that gives you no right to . . .

GEORGES. No rights at all, Mme Guillaume, I know—(*he sits her on the sofa*) but listen to me. (*He sits beside her*) You seem to be quite a nice old lady—

PROPRIETRESS (*wondering what is behind all this*) Oh, I'm not at all—really . . .

GEORGES. —what's more, you have a charming old house, but you never manage to let it, do you? Now, I've paid you quite a high price to have this place for a month.

PROPRIETRESS (*plaintively*) I wanted to let it for the year.

GEORGES (*amused*) And I wanted to take it for the year. We all want to do things by the year, Mme Guillaume, but we can never manage them for more than a week, sometimes only a day. That's what life's like.

PROPRIETRESS. A day! Oh, no! Never! It's humiliating enough already to let by the month. (*She attempts to rise*)

(GEORGES *restrains her*)

I'm not a boarding-house landlady.

GEORGES (*seriously*) You're too finicky, Mme Guillaume. Anyway, I'd be the happiest man alive, if I could live in your house a whole month.

PROPRIETRESS. There's nothing to stop you. You've paid until the first of July.

GEORGES. Yes, I know. But I shall only stay here for one night. Tonight.

PROPRIETRESS. It's nothing to do with me, but what I don't understand is—

GEORGES. What?

ACT I   DINNER WITH THE FAMILY

PROPRIETRESS. —why a young man who lives alone should need a large house like this, miles away from Paris, buried in the country . . .

GEORGES (*rising and moving* C) I have to entertain relations. (*He moves to the sofa*) Incidentally—I am sure you will understand—it would be rather embarrassing for me to have to explain to—er—these relations—that I only moved in this evening. Would you be very kind and stay upstairs in your room?

(*The* PROPRIETRESS *rises*)

(*He helps her to rise*) And do please hide this inventory somewhere.

PROPRIETRESS (*moving above the sofa*) I'll leave you the copy. You can check it over tomorrow when you have more time.

GEORGES (*moving up* C) I'll do my best with it.

PROPRIETRESS. May I say that I make a point of never disturbing my tenants. (*She moves to the telephone*) Ah, I forgot—you can't use this telephone. It hasn't any wires, you see. It's a souvenir. (*She indicates the armchair up* C) Oh, and be careful of this chair; one leg is broken. If your relatives are heavy people, you'd do better to give them the sofa. (*She moves to the window*) Be careful of the window, too, the glass is fragile. There are sixty-three separate panes—one of them's just been re-glued. This one.

GEORGES (*resigned*) This one's re-glued. I'll guard it with my life.

PROPRIETRESS (*suddenly pointing* L *with a feverish finger*) Oh, look there—(*she crosses to* L) to the left of that candelabra.

(GEORGES *follows the Proprietress*)

Wouldn't you say that looks rather like a bird?

GEORGES (*pitilessly*) No.

(*The* PROPRIETRESS *sighs and goes into the hall*)

PROPRIETRESS (*reading her inventory*) "Trees, flowers *and birds.*"

(*The front door bell rings. The* PROPRIETRESS *turns to go to the front door*)

GEORGES (*moving quickly into the hall*) That's for me. I'll open the door myself.

PROPRIETRESS. But won't your relatives think it odd, your living in this big house without any servants?

GEORGES. Thank you. I've thought of that.

(*The* PROPRIETRESS *exits up the stairs.*

    GEORGES *exits* L *in the hall. He re-enters the hall carrying a small attaché case, crosses and exits* R *in the hall to open the front door*)

BUTLER (*off*) M. Delachaume?

GEORGES (*off*) Yes, that's me. Do come in.

BUTLER (*off*) Jean Dufort at your service.

(GEORGES *enters the hall from* R *and comes into the room.*
EMILE, *the* BUTLER, *follows him on*)

GEORGES. Dufort's do things promptly; it's scarcely an hour since I telephoned. (*He goes to the sofa, puts the attaché case on it, extracts a book and puts it on the sofa seat*)

BUTLER (*moving* C) We always have a few choice dinners in readiness, sir. It just means putting the dishes into a van and off we go. My assistants are in the kitchen already, sir. The champagne is on ice, the claret at the right temperature. In a quarter of an hour dinner can be served. (*He recites*)

> Nothing warmed up, all quite hot,
> Time and distance trouble not.
> A miracle, just one more,
> From the firm of Jean *Dufort*

(*He bows*)

GEORGES (*picking up the case and moving to* R *of the Butler*) Do you believe in them?

BUTLER. In what, sir?

GEORGES. Miracles.

BUTLER (*changing his tone*) No, sir. Still, Dufort's is one of the best organized and best . . .

(GEORGES *takes a thousand franc note from his pocket and gives it to the Butler*)

GEORGES. How old is the vol-au-vent which is "never warmed up, always hot"? (*He crosses to the piano, sits on the stool, takes some manuscript music from the case and puts it on the piano*)

BUTLER (*modestly*) Oh, sir, beautifully mature. If you have any little pets, sir, they're usually fond of the crust—as for the sauce, well . . . (*He makes a vague gesture*)

GEORGES. I see we understand each other. Serve what you are sure of and that's all. And don't let it look too much like a banquet. Now, there's one special thing that may sound rather odd, I suppose, to you. Please don't serve anything that obviously comes from Dufort's. (*He takes a photograph of himself from the case and puts it on the piano*)

BUTLER (*crossing to* R *of Georges*) I don't quite follow, sir.

GEORGES. Listen. I've had to improvise this meal. I turned to a caterer because I had so little time, but, so far as my guests are concerned, everything has been cooked here in the house. Do you follow me, now?

BUTLER. Perfectly, sir.

GEORGES. What are your assistants like? Pretty rough-looking individuals?

BUTLER (*with scorn*) Just assistants, sir.

GEORGES. Don't have them too much in evidence.

ACT I   DINNER WITH THE FAMILY   7

BUTLER. I intended to keep them out in any case, sir. One because of his smell, sir, and the other has a glass eye.
GEORGES. In the kitchen, definitely. I want very simple service. Nothing *Dufort* about it. Is that clear?
BUTLER. Very well, sir, but . . .
GEORGES (*giving him another thousand francs*) But what?
BUTLER (*quickly pocketing the note*) There is no "but".
GEORGES. Have you always been a hired butler?
BUTLER (*wounded*) One is not born so, sir, one becomes it in self-defence. I was seventeen years with the Duke of Maine, sir.
GEORGES. What made you leave him?
BUTLER (*flattered*) You are very kind to suppose that it was I who left, sir. It was the Duke who had to leave me.
GEORGES. Ruined?
BUTLER. Yes, sir, er—physically, through abuse, sir. His heart was finished; kidneys refused to function; the arteries, sir, just a lot of old piping; the spleen all torn to shreds . . .
GEORGES. Spare me the full description. The main thing is that you have been in a well-to-do household. (*He rises and puts the case on the stool*) What is your name?
BUTLER. Graduzac.
GEORGES. I meant your Christian name.
BUTLER. Emile. But the custom, sir, with a hired butler is . . .
GEORGES. Emile, what I want is not customary; that is precisely the point. You are a man with imagination, I can see. Now—picture yourself dandling me on your knees.
BUTLER (*backing to* G) Me, sir?
GEORGES. Yes, Emile.
BUTLER (*embarrassed*) I don't know if you realize, sir, that I am getting on in years and nothing in my appearance could lead anyone to suppose . . .
GEORGES (*moving to the Butler*) Emile! Please! We are at cross purposes. The thing I'm asking is very simple and quite respectable. I want you to say, not that you are hired but that you are the permanent butler in this house. Is that clear?
BUTLER. Yes, sir. In nine cases out of ten, sir, vanity rules people's lives.
GEORGES. Well, that's the first point. Next, Emile, I think you've always been here, since my childhood. Would it be asking too much for you to have been here when I was born?
BUTLER. It would be an honour, sir. An honour and a pleasure. I adore babies.
GEORGES (*moving to the piano*) It's too late for the pleasure, I'm afraid. (*He picks up the attaché case and puts it behind the screen*) But take the honour, by all means.
BUTLER. Delighted. Henceforth, I say that I was here when you were born, sir.

GEORGES. Right. And you dandled me on your knee when I was—(*he gestures*) no bigger than that.
BUTLER (*with relief*) No bigger than that—the size makes all the difference.
GEORGES (*moving to him*) How much did I give you just now?
BUTLER. I have forgotten, sir—it is a principle with me.
GEORGES. Good. If I give you twice that amount to play the old family butler during dinner this evening, will that be all right?
BUTLER. Could you go, sir, to another five thousand?
GEORGES. Done! (*He gives the Butler a five thousand franc note*)
BUTLER (*suddenly warming up*) In that case, I've been with the family for years, sir. And my father was butler here before me. I worked in the kitchen when I was young, then went off to various parts of the world to learn the business; and, when my father had to retire, I came back to take his place.
GEORGES (*crossing above the sofa to* R) Fine! But don't embroider too much. I shall be introducing you to my parents in a moment.
BUTLER. Won't your parents be rather surprised, sir?
GEORGES (*smiling*) Not in the least—don't worry.

(*The front door bell rings*)

Emile. Go and let my parents in, will you?
BUTLER (*moving towards the hall*) Certainly, baron.
GEORGES (*with a start*) What?
BUTLER (*stopping and turning*) Don't you think I should give you a title while we are about it, sir?
GEORGES (*crossing to the Butler*) Listen, Emile. I'm not trying to put the grand family across—not that at all. Old retainer, simple and honest, almost one of the family, that's your line. If I hadn't been pressed for time I would probably have preferred an old Breton nursemaid.
BUTLER (*reproachfully*) Oh, sir! Breton nursemaids are overdone—ten a penny, sir. No one with real taste, sir, would ever . . .
GEORGES. Anyway, simplicity's the keynote—no title. Do you see?
BUTLER. As you wish, sir. There is one point, though—are we in your house, sir, or in your—er—parents' house?
GEORGES. My parents' house.

(*The front door bell rings again*)

BUTLER. In that case would you be so good as to tell me your first name, sir? Custom requires that I call your father simply "Monsieur", and you yourself "M. Jean" or "M. Lucien" or "M. . . .?"
GEORGES (*cutting in*) "Georges."
BUTLER. M. Georges. (*He repeats it*) M. Georges. Good. I must get it well into my head. (*He gravely repeats*) M. Georges. That's

ACT I DINNER WITH THE FAMILY 9

right. Now, I'd better answer the bell. What room should I show them to, M. Georges?
GEORGES (*exasperated*) Straight in here, Emile.

(*The* BUTLER *exits in the hall to* R. GEORGES *hovers above the sofa*)

BUTLER (*off*) What name shall I say?
MME DE MONTRACHET (*off*) Mme de Montrachet.
DELMONTE (*off*) M. Delmonte.

(*The* BUTLER *enters from the hall and stands to* L *of the doorway*)

BUTLER (*announcing*) Mme de Montrachet and M. Delmonte.

(MME DE MONTRACHET *and* DELMONTE *enter from the hall.* DELMONTE *carries a small attaché case which he puts on the floor* L *of the doorway*)

GEORGES (*moving to them*) Very glad to see you. You are very punctual. Did you come together? (*He crosses below the sofa to* R)

(*The* BUTLER *exits to the hall, closing the doors behind him*)

DELMONTE. We met at the station. We used to be the best of friends, inseparable, only we've lost sight of one another, for ten years or more. Imagine our surprise. I rushed up to her with arms outstretched, almost speechless.

(MME DE MONTRACHET *and* DELMONTE *mime their meeting on the spot*)

"Emilienne! Darling!"
MME DE MONTRACHET. "Ferdinand! Darling! Fancy running into you like this. All those years of touring together and we've never clapped eyes on each other since."
DELMONTE. "Well, Emilienne! This brings back all those wonderful tours in Egypt and Algeria. Do you remember? *Saint Joan* at Ben Said and *Romeo* at Hafi Moufa?" Oh! "Do I remember that *Romeo*? You were magnificent, Ferdinand, dear. The way they cheered. And most of them couldn't understand a word, could they?" And so forth and so on . . . "But—where are you going, darling?" I said. "Where are *you*, Ferdinand, dear?" she said.
MME DE MONTRACHET. "Thirty-two rue Victor," he said. "So am I," I said. "Not to a young gentleman's house? What's his name? Delachaume? Some mystery about it?"
DELMONTE. "Both of us? No. Oh, it's too fantastic. Come, let's go together."

(MME DE MONTRACHET *and* DELMONTE *cross arm-in-arm to* GEORGES)

And off we started arm-in-arm like in the old days.

GEORGES. Good!
DELMONTE. Wait, wait, though. As we came into the Place Clemenceau, Emilienne suddenly stops, so I say: "What's the matter, my dear? Have you forgotten something?" She squeezes my arm. "Ferdinand, we've acted in this town together before. A very long time ago."
MME DE MONTRACHET. It was uncanny. I felt certain I was wearing ankle-length bloomers. (*To Georges*) I'm not, of course.
GEORGES. Of course not.
DELMONTE. Then I say sceptically: "There's a Place Clemenceau in nearly every town in France, darling." "But something tells me . . ." And suddenly she cried out: "Look at that statue."
MME DE MONTRACHET (*with a gesture*) Ah! That statue!
DELMONTE. I look at the statue; and stand rooted to the ground . . .
GEORGES (*interrupting*) You had played here before?
DELMONTE (*very simply*) No, it was a mistake.
GEORGES. Forgive me. I'd love to hear the rest of the story, but I have so much to get ready this evening, and very little time ahead of me.
DELMONTE. When Guillotard first spoke of this engagement, he said Tuesday *or* Wednesday . . .
GEORGES. My plans were changed at the last minute. I need your help tonight. Do sit down, and I'll explain what I want you to do.

(DELMONTE *and* MME DE MONTRACHET *sit on the sofa.* GEORGES *crosses to* C)

MME DE MONTRACHET. Yes, of course—I'm most intrigued. What is it all about?
DELMONTE. Guillotard is a very old friend of yours, isn't he, my dear? *He* gave us to understand it was something out of the ordinary.
GEORGES. Yes. I suppose it is.
DELMONTE (*with the indulgence of a man quite used to the caprices of amateurs*) Very well, we are listening, my dear sir.
MME DE MONTRACHET. We are all ears. (*She laughs*) Do you remember, darling, how he used to say that every time we had a reading? Old Gado, you know, the stage manager at the *Ambigu Theatre*?
DELMONTE (*laughing*) Oh, yes. Good Lord! (*He laughs*) What's happened to old Gado?
MME DE MONTRACHET. What! Haven't you heard? He's dead.
DELMONTE. No? Old Gado?
MME DE MONTRACHET. Yes. "We are all ears." Ha! Ha! Been dead some time. (*She roars with laughter*)

(DELMONTE *laughs till the tears roll down his cheeks*)

DELMONTE. "We are all ears, all ears." My God, he was a comic chap. (*He suddenly turns sad*) Poor old Gado.

(MME DE MONTRACHET *suddenly stops laughing*)

MME DE MONTRACHET. Poor old Gado.

(*They turn together towards Georges, with quite expressionless faces*)

GEORGES (*a little surprised*) Well, now—I haven't brought you here to act a play in a theatre . . .

DELMONTE (*cutting in quickly*) One moment. I'm sorry, but I must butt in there. It's not for the films, I hope?

GEORGES. No, no, nothing to do with films. (*He sits on the right arm of the armchair* LC *and lights a cigarette*)

DELMONTE (*turning to Mme de Montrachet*) I've just finished a few days' filming with Bourbenski. They'll never get me at that again. Those fellows on the other side of the Atlantic are born in it and have grown a sixth sense by now, but *I* am a theatre animal. Human contact, real human contact, that's the thing.

MME DE MONTRACHET. I'm just the same. I must feel them there, vibrating in front of me; their tears, their laughter, ready to flow at the artist's touch. My audience. Difficult, unpredictable, human. It makes me think of taming a mule—a wild, stubborn, rebellious mule. That reminds me, darling, is your health any better since we were at Biarritz?

DELMONTE. Health? My dear, with all their films and things, I can't steal a minute to think of my health. (*He suddenly remembers Georges and turns to him*) Oh, forgive us. Let's get back to the point. As our old stage manager always used to say: "We are all ears."

(*They both break into laughter again, then suddenly stop*)

Poor old Gado.

MME DE MONTRACHET (*with a sigh*) Poor old Gado.

GEORGES (*rising and moving to* L *of the sofa; somewhat annoyed*) I'm afraid I must have your full attention, now. In half an hour my guests will be here and you must know your parts by then.

DELMONTE. Pardon me! I hope you've no intention of asking us to play parts we've not yet read?

GEORGES. Yes, I have.

DELMONTE. But the script? Where are our lines?

GEORGES. There are no words for you to learn.

MME DE MONTRACHET. Oh. We're not expected to improvise?

GEORGES. Don't get alarmed before you know what I'm asking of you, please. To tell you the truth—(*he moves up* C) I turned to professional actors so that I'd have every possible guarantee of success. What you have to do is very simple, almost anybody could pull it off.

DELMONTE. Amateurs, eh? Well, sir, I can't do more than wish some on you.
GEORGES. Well, isn't this simple? I want you to have dinner here this evening and keep up as interesting a conversation as possible with my guests.
DELMONTE (*rising; delighted*) Ah, now I understand. I think you might go a long way with that scheme, you know. As a matter of fact, I had the same idea myself, some time ago. Original, Emilienne, isn't it? Most original. If I understand you, sir, you're having a dinner party, and you're afraid of its being rather flat. So you mix with your guests a few persons, whose profession, and exceptional gifts, make them more interesting, more brilliant, more . . .
GEORGES (*interrupting*) Not exactly. (*He moves to* L *of the sofa*) I have no doubts about your charm, or your wit. But what I really want to appeal to is your professional skill, your ability to imitate special traits in other people's characters and make them appear absolutely natural to you.
DELMONTE. Ah! There you are! If we didn't have that talent we'd be knocking nails into shoes or polishing ball-bearings, I suppose—like everybody else.
MME DE MONTRACHET. It's the gift, you see. Either it's there— or it's not.
GEORGES (*sitting in the armchair* LC) That's why I want you to help me. I spoke of "my guests" just now, I really mean "my guest". I am expecting a young lady at almost any minute. Let me be quite frank with you—for reasons which it would take too long to explain, I found myself lying to this young lady. Oh, nothing serious, really. All my lies can be put in a sentence or two. My real parents are dead, and I told her they were still alive and lived just outside Paris. Why? Why did I tell her that? (*Throughout the following, he is obviously improvising*) Well, for a very simple reason. Just to explain away my absences during the week. I was involved with someone else—an old affaire I could not bring myself to tell her about . . . That's not all. Actually, I have no friends. But you must know how weak a man in love can be.
DELMONTE. Oh, do I know!
MME DE MONTRACHET. And women, too.
GEORGES. When this young lady, who is pure and innocent and has deep faith in friendship, when she said one day how amazed she was that a man of my age had no friends—I just invented one, whole, so as not to disappoint her. And, of course, while I was at it, I made a good job of it. I made him the best friend in the world; brave, sincere, devoted. I only wanted to please her, you see—so there was no need to be niggardly about it.
DELMONTE. Ah love! Love! I've spun a few yarns in my time, too. Once in Marseilles I made a little waitress believe I was an

international soccer player. (*He moves up* c, *miming a footballer*) Ha! (*He rocks with laughter*) An outside left.

GEORGES (*going on without taking any notice*) I had no idea what a mistake I was making when I invented these people. The girl got into the habit of asking after them. Then, of course, I was forced to invent more and more things about them; they interested her and she began to wonder why I didn't let her meet them—as they meant so much to me. For a long time I put her off with excuses; they were ill, or out of town; but tomorrow she's leaving for her home in the country for the summer. I can't hold back any longer. So I've asked her here to dinner this evening to meet my parents, *and* the friend I've talked so much about.

DELMONTE (*sitting on the left arm of the sofa*) I'm beginning to see daylight. You want us to be the parents?

GEORGES. Yes. And to talk as they would talk if they really existed.

DELMONTE. Wonderful!

MME DE MONTRACHET. Oh, splendid! I think it's too marvellous for words.

DELMONTE. Isn't it? But, tell me, who's playing the friend?

GEORGES. I didn't want an actor for that. Parents are straight forward enough to play. They always talk to their son's girl about the comic things he used to say at eighteen months, and the alarming way he shot up in his teens. She doesn't get any more out of them than that. But not a friend. There are so many things a woman can ask him. We'll lay a place for him and wait dinner for him as long as common courtesy requires. But his chair will stay empty. (*To himself. Softly*) That way he stands a chance of remaining a perfect friend.

(*There is a short silence*)

DELMONTE. I'm sorry about that. I know a very talented youngster who would have done fine for the part.

GEORGES (*smiling*) I don't think so.

MME DE MONTRACHET. I'm just too thrilled with the idea of playing the mother. Mothers are always magnificent parts. Especially when one is still a young woman, don't you think? There's something irresistible about a young mother.

GEORGES (*rising and moving to* L *of the sofa*) Yes, but don't let your imagination run on until we've gone over things together. As you can guess, I've talked to her in detail about you, so you'll have to call on every bit of talent you have. You have to bring to life, in flesh and blood, the exact characters that I've already planted in her mind.

DELMONTE (*rising*) Oh, wait! Wait a minute, old chap. I've got an idea for a rattling good father. (*He moves up* LC *and picks up his attaché case*) Just a minute, I've got all I need for it here.

(DELMONTE, *before* GEORGES *can make a move, darts behind the screen* L)

MME DE MONTRACHET (*coyly*) So here am I with a big boy of my own. A big boy I just adore, or don't I? I hope you haven't cast me for a bad mother. I should be quite unable to play it.

GEORGES. An excellent mother. You dote on your son.

MME DE MONTRACHET. Guillotard told me to wear a black dress. This one has a *touch* of colour. But she's not in mourning, is she?

GEORGES. No.

MME DE MONTRACHET. You know, the essential thing in playing a young mother is to give the feeling that, in spite of everything, she is still very feminine.

GEORGES (*sitting beside Mme de Montrachet on the sofa*) No, please! It's just the opposite I want. We mustn't feel that at all.

MME DE MONTRACHET (*crossly*) Well, just as you like. But, with my looks, you must see I can't play an old hag.

GEORGES. Be patient just a little longer, please, and we'll go into your character in detail.

(DELMONTE *emerges from the screen and crosses to* L *of the sofa. He is disguised as a wrinkled and bearded old man, doubled up with age*)

What the . . .?

DELMONTE. It's me! Ha, ha, ha, ha! That's very funny. He was caught in the trap himself.

GEORGES (*in consternation*) You're not going to sit down to dinner like that, I hope?

DELMONTE. No, no, don't worry. I shall do it all again, better. This was only to give you an idea of the general effect.

GEORGES. But it's impossible! You've misunderstood me, I can see.

DELMONTE (*suddenly flying into a temper*) What the devil! You told me a father character. I produce a father for you. You're not going to stand there and pretend you can teach me my job, damn it all!

GEORGES (*rising*) No—but—that's out of the question. I'm sorry, but it's miles away from what I . . .

DELMONTE (*heatedly*) Let's get this straight. Do you want a romantic young lead or do you want a father? I understood you wanted a father and *this is* a father.

GEORGES (*rising and moving up* C) Tell me, how old are you, in reality, M. Delmonte? (*He comes down* C)

DELMONTE. Fifty-two, and thirty-four years on the stage. So you're not talking to a mere call-boy, remember.

MME DE MONTRACHET (*rising and crossing to Delmonte; trying to calm him*) Ferdinand—Ferdinand, don't upset yourself, darling.

GEORGES. You are fifty-two and I'm twenty-eight. So in all seriousness it's no violation of nature to pass you off as my father without false whiskers.

DELMONTE (*tearing his beard off in a fury*) Oh! Well! I was a fool to go to so much trouble. If you want somebody with the looks of a leading man to play the part of the father straight—don't let me stop you. Anyway, the success of the whole business is no-one's concern but your own—but I insist on your knowing that I'm giving way simply because this is a young man's whim. And no more! It's unimportant! (*He goes behind the screen*)

(GEORGES *moves to the table up* C *and stubs out his cigarette in the ashtray*)

I have a respect for my profession, sir, deep respect. (*He emerges from the screen, carrying his attaché case which he puts on the floor by the piano*) If there'd been any artistic principle at stake, the boot would have been on the other foot, I can tell you.

GEORGES (*sharply*) I didn't bring you here just to play-act. (*He moves to* R *of the chair* LC) These characters exist. They're already half alive. Someone believes in them—and expects special words, special gestures from them: a special atmosphere around me. You—you cling to your professional conscience—well, it must make you obey me as unquestioningly as you would the most finicky producer in the theatre. You must help me with all the talent you have. We have to bring to life the father, mother and friend that this young girl is expecting to see.

(*The* ACTORS *are surprised by his tone*)

(*He moves down* R) You probably think I'm crazy. You're used to the sort of theatre where the different kinds of play never get mixed up—and here you find a young man with a sad face and trembling hands pushing you into a farce instead of a tragedy. Some people seem to carry tragedy at their finger-tips—given only half a situation, a leave-taking, a mere hint of pain, they can turn on the tears in a moment and draw them from the onlookers, too. It so happens that I'm not made that way. I always have to play my life as a farce. (*He crosses to* C) So help me, will you? Help me bring these people to life just for one evening. I'm more anxious to see them than any man has ever been to see his real father and mother, or his real best friend, even after years of separation.

(*The* ACTORS *cough, moved by his words*)

MME DE MONTRACHET. You know how sentimental we women are—we're always ready to help lovers . . .

DELMONTE. We are at your disposal, sir. Aren't we, Emilienne? And—er—I'm sorry for my show of temper just now . . .

GEORGES (*with a gesture to stop them*) Thank you. But, please, from now on don't speak another word as your real selves. (*He leads Mme de Montrachet to the sofa*) We must begin at once.

(MME DE MONTRACHET *sits on the sofa*)

We have so little time and so much to learn. (*He sits on the sofa*) One thing particularly will be difficult, I feel—achieving the exact degree of restraint that comes of long-standing affection, the sort of intimate silence I've always envied in people who understand one another so well they have no need of words.

DELMONTE (*moving to* L *of the sofa*) My dear sir, silence is the easiest thing to do in the theatre. I think you should tell us a few of the other things that matter, first.

GEORGES. All right. (*He rises*) Why did you imagine yourself wearing a beard like an old crank out of a museum? You're really a very charming man, still quite young, with a youth that time cannot touch. You're the ideal father, you have no patriarchal manner. You're much more of an elder brother. You are my friend, Father. What's more, you dress like me, you even dress younger—but that's natural at your age.

DELMONTE. Still you know—for a father . . .? (*He shrugs*)

GEORGES (*with a smile*) Of course, Father—there *are* times when a normal elder brother would think of himself first; when it's a question of making a sacrifice, or of lending a bit of money—that's when you turn into a real father again, strong and comforting, the sort a fellow can still act the little boy with for a moment, and not feel embarrassed.

DELMONTE. Yes, Son.

GEORGES (*happily*) There, you see, it's true. You've called me "Son". It's a bit ridiculous and I didn't tell you to, of course, but I like it.

DELMONTE (*putting a hand on Georges' shoulder*) Really?

GEORGES. Yes, Father.

DELMONTE (*moving down* R *of the piano; with a change of tone*) You don't think the expression rather too sentimental for a retired judge?

GEORGES. But you've never been a judge. Where did you get that idea?

DELMONTE. Just came to me. I would have quite liked being a retired judge.

GEORGES (*crossing to Delmonte*) No, no. You're not a judge, Father, couldn't be. You always needed at least three weeks when we caught the maid pilfering to give her the sack. Even then you always gave her a glowing testimonial. I can't see you packing two or three dozen poor devils off to gaol every day and then calmly sitting down to afternoon tea.

DELMONTE (*crossing and sitting in the chair* LC) What am I, then, Son? A chain-store owner, stockbroker, powerful industrialist?

GEORGES. No. People who spend their whole lives piling up

money pick up such dreadful habits. No. You may be a civil servant. I can see you quite well in that sort of work.

DELMONTE (*troubled*) Not some silly little pen-pusher, I hope? You'll at least put me in one of the upper grades of the service?

GEORGES (*generously*) Of course. I'll even make you a—First Secretary.

DELMONTE (*overwhelmed*) Oh, thanks.

MME DE MONTRACHET (*annoyed and sulky*) Nothing's been said about me.

(GEORGES *crosses to* MME DE MONTRACHET *and sits beside her on the sofa*)

GEORGES (*suddenly serious*) Ah, yours is the more difficult part. There's such a range in mothers. From the grey-wigged tyrant, dearly defending her heritage, to the sweet and anxious lady, who trembles like a young girl in love and loses the thread of the conversation whenever her son comes into the room.

MME DE MONTRACHET. A good mother's part ought to range over them all.

GEORGES. No, I want this one to be quite straightforward. Clear. Like one of those mothers in children's books. The sort little boys *dream* about as they wait in the kitchen with the maids, while their *real* mother—drenched in perfume—is out on one of those interminable afternoon calls. A mother who doesn't make trips to the shops all the time, and has no friends to visit. A wonderful mother.

MME DE MONTRACHET. All mothers are wonderful, instinct tells me so.

GEORGES. The slightest sign of neglect can ruin all that. An unguarded smile to a strange man. A harsh word at the end of a trying day. A simple kiss forgotten just when it's due. And there you have a child watching you, making demands on you, as big a tyrant as a sergeant-major. I know it's not easy to play the mother. It's a part that can have no understudy and that should never be taken on light-heartedly.

MME DE MONTRACHET. I'm quite familiar with mother parts— all sorts. You should have seen my "mother" in *Brittany First*.

DELMONTE. Ah, my dear, yes. You were delightful.

GEORGES. I don't trust stage-mothers. Their devotion is much too facile.

MME DE MONTRACHET. Oh, but I've played wicked mothers, too. In *She Was Guilty*, for instance, I abandoned my baby on the steps of the church.

GEORGES. Exactly. I don't trust wicked stage-mothers, either. They're laid on too thick. With them a real child wouldn't have time to be unhappy. He'd be dead or turned into a lunatic straight away. In the first place, would anybody think of leaving a baby on the steps of a church when there are so many easier ways of abandoning a child? Some women can do it by just keeping him at home until he's of age.

MME DE MONTRACHET. Well . . . If you think I shan't be able to play the part . . .

DELMONTE. No need for me to say, young man, that if that is the case, I shall be forced to leave with my colleague.

GEORGES. What makes you think that? I'm convinced you'll play it very well. Just to give us confidence if you like, we'll have a little rehearsal. (*He rises and moves up* C) Let's play one scene, a typical scene. Imagine I am twenty, I'm a weak young man, easily led, not very good at facing up to life. Let us suppose, to get a situation, that you have arranged a rich marriage for me. (*He repeats this, suddenly very far away*) A very rich marriage, a pure business deal, something you, my mother, ought never to have considered. I've just come into your room. I've talked about one or two things, then suddenly, awkward and embarrassed, I come up to you and say: "Mother . . ." (*He sits beside Mme de Montrachet on the sofa*) Come, have a try, let's play the scene together.

DELMONTE (*leaping to his feet and crossing to Georges*) One moment, one moment, Emilienne de Montrachet, you're one of the oldest members of the Union, are you going to agree to an audition *after* being engaged for the job?

MME DE MONTRACHET. It's not quite the same, Ferdinand. I just want to convince this gentleman that . . .

DELMONTE (*crossing to the piano and leaning on it, facing* L) As you please, darling—but—it's not like you at all. That's all I can say.

GEORGES. Well, "Mother" . . .

MME DE MONTRACHET. Shall I answer you?

GEORGES. Yes.

MME DE MONTRACHET (*playing her part*) What is it, dear?

(GEORGES *answers with his eyes closed and in a curious voice. One feels one no longer knows to whom he is speaking*)

GEORGES. Mother—I don't want to marry the girl you've chosen for me, however rich she may be. Being rich doesn't mean anything to me, Mother. I'm in love with someone else. (*He goes on to his knees*) She's poor and has to earn her own living, and I know you won't want me to marry her. But I must. I can't marry anyone else. Please help me.

(MME DE MONTRACHET, *surprised by his tone perhaps, hesitates.* GEORGES *listens in silence, with closed eyes*)

MME DE MONTRACHET (*rather nobly*) I thought I was doing the right thing, dear. But if your happiness is really somewhere else, you mustn't hesitate; go and be happy. At your age, love is *the one thing* that counts and that cannot be bought. (*She pauses, then changes her tone. A bit anxious*) Was that all right?

GEORGES (*opening his eyes; as if surprised*) I'm sorry. It's very good. In fact, it's exactly what the mother I've imagined would have said. Congratulations! (*He rises*) Is that a speech from one of your other parts?

MME DE MONTRACHET. No, I made it up.

GEORGES. It couldn't have been better. Just as if you had a son who'd already asked you the same question.

MME DE MONTRACHET (*simpering*) Well, yes—I admit I have. You wouldn't think so, would you, looking as young as I do? A grown-up son. He came to me with exactly the same story a year ago; so, of course, I was rehearsed, in a way.

GEORGES (*looking at her, full of admiration*) And that's the answer you gave him?

MME DE MONTRACHET (*suddenly carried away at the recollection*) A tuppeny violinist! A flibberty-gibbet without a sou to her name. I soon knocked all that nonsense out of his head, I can tell you.

GEORGES (*sitting on the sofa; smiling*) No! Please. Be the same as you were a few moments ago. There, that's it. Now that you've put your own child out of your mind, you make quite a wonderful mother again. (*He rises and moves* C) This girl may arrive at any moment—so get yourselves used to the room. You've been living here for thirty years, remember. Look round for the odd little things in it that specially belong to you, that reflect you individually. Mother, have you a bit of knitting with you for instance?

MME DE MONTRACHET (*taking some knitting from her bag*) I always carry some; there's such a lot of waiting in the agents' offices.

GEORGES. Father, get your newspaper out. You've got one with you, I imagine?

DELMONTE. Two. *La Vie Parisienne* and *Figaro*. (*He takes the newspapers from his attaché case, then puts the case behind the screen and sits in the armchair* LC) I found them on my way here; they were lying on the seat in the train.

GEORGES. Grand! They're both indispensable signs of a decent middle-class life. But remember you must make a show of reading *Figaro*, and you can only take a peep at *La Vie Parisienne* now and then on the sly. (*The tableau is now set. He steps back, narrowing his eyes like a painter*) There—you don't dislike each other, you know, you're a very devoted couple. It wouldn't be overdoing it to bring your chairs a little closer to each other.

(DELMONTE *moves his chair nearer to the sofa*)

That's it. Fine.

DELMONTE (*suddenly feeling in his pockets*) Damn, I was forgetting . . .

GEORGES. What's that?

DELMONTE. Nothing, a minor point, just a little touch, but I like to have the details right in any character. It's the Legion of Honour for my buttonhole. (*He takes the rosette from his pocket and fixes it to his lapel*)

(GEORGES *looks at the others for a moment in silence, then sits on the sofa*)

GEORGES. It's very strange, and somehow very comforting, bringing all these lies to life.

(*In the silence a clock strikes eight, with a musical chime. The light begins to fade as the sun sets*)

Eight o'clock. She'll be here in a second. Ah, I was forgetting. Can you play the piano, Mother? I specially asked M. Guillotard for someone who played the piano.

MME DE MONTRACHET. I won the Napoleon Bronze Medal at the Dieppe Academy in nineteen-twenty-five.

(GEORGES *and* MME DE MONTRACHET *rise and cross to the piano*)

GEORGES. Splendid. You'll manage this piece quite easily.

(MME DE MONTRACHET *sits at the piano*)

It's a tune I heard one evening when I was only ten years old. I was wandering through the streets alone—suddenly I heard music coming from an open window. I stood up on a wall and peeped through. In an old-fashioned sitting-room, rather like this, a little girl with plaits was playing the piano—and the whole family sat round listening.

MME DE MONTRACHET (*trying out the piece softly on the piano*) It's a waltz, by Oliver Metra.

GEORGES (*crossing slowly above the sofa and standing down* R) As soon as I met the young lady who's coming tonight, I went round all the music-shops singing that tune, until someone recognized it. I had to sing it for two months. I'm tone-deaf, you see, so I had to be very patient—so did the salesmen in the music shops, of course.

(*The* BUTLER *enters from the hall and crosses to* R *of the sofa*)

BUTLER. Excuse me, sir. I know your order was for four persons, but sometimes—since people know that we do things on a quite generous scale at Dufort's . . . Well, to come to the point, how many should I lay for?

GEORGES. Five.

BUTLER. Just as I thought. Very well, sir. (*He crosses to the hall; muttering*) They're all the same.

GEORGES (*following the Butler*) Emile! There'll only be four of us to dinner in spite of that. The fifth person won't be eating.

(*The* BUTLER, *astonished at first, thinks he understands. He is charmed and most impressed with this touch*)

BUTLER. Ah! I ask your pardon, sir. It's the poor man's place, no doubt?

(GEORGES *looks at the Butler*)

At the Duke's, where all the traditions were respected, we always laid an extra place on special occasions, for the poor. A poor man was always welcome at the Duke's table.

GEORGES. And did a poor man come, now and then?

BUTLER. No, sir, never. His place was laid, but as no one ever took the trouble to inform him of it—poor man . . .

(*The* BUTLER, *very dignified, exits with a cynical gesture to the hall.* MME DE MONTRACHET *rises and moves towards the sofa.* DELMONTE *rises and catches her arm*)

DELMONTE. We were fools. We ought to have asked for a larger fee.

(*The front door bell rings twice*)

GEORGES. Two rings, that'll be Isabelle. I told her to give two rings. In your places, quickly. You, Mother, at the piano. And start playing.

(MME DE MONTRACHET *sits at the piano*)

(*He moves below the sofa*) You, Father, there, behind.

(DELMONTE *sits in the chair* LC)

(*He sits on the sofa and picks up his book*) I am reading. Be careful what you say, keep your imagination well under control, don't let it run away with you. And keep your eye on me. I shall cut in as soon as anything gets too dangerous. Anyway, you know enough now to play your parts.

(MME DE MONTRACHET *commences to play*)

There's no need for any hitches if you are careful.

MME DE MONTRACHET (*stopping playing abruptly*) And you? What about you?

GEORGES. How do you mean?

MME DE MONTRACHET. She's sure to ask us about you. You've told us nothing about yourself. Your character, your history.

GEORGES (*rising and rushing to the hall door*) Good God, that's true. (*He calls*) Emile! Emile!

(*The* BUTLER *enters from the hall*)

BUTLER. I was just going to answer the bell, sir.

GEORGES. It's the young lady I'm expecting. Take your time

going to the door—and bringing her up here. Take as much time as you can.

(*The* BUTLER *exits very slowly in the hall to* R)

(*He moves down* L) Listen carefully, both of you. Ah! I haven't got time to tell you much.

(*The* BUTLER *enters hurriedly from the hall*)

BUTLER (*very upset*) Please, sir, please, sir.
GEORGES. What is it?
BUTLER. I've forgotten your Christian name.
GEORGES (*shouting*) Georges.
BUTLER. M. Georges, that's it. It'll stick this time.

(*The* BUTLER *rushes, remembers—then slowly exits*)

GEORGES (*to the others*) My name is Georges, my friend's is Jacques.
MME DE MONTRACHET }(*together*) Yes.
DELMONTE
GEORGES (*moving nervously up* C) I'm very shy. Start playing.
MME DE MONTRACHET. Very well. (*She plays the waltz softly*)
GEORGES. I'm practical—no imagination.
DELMONTE. Hm!
GEORGES. I'm good-humoured, a bit countrified, rash now and then, generous, kind.
DELMONTE. Good.
GEORGES. I was a wild and cruel little boy, but when anybody even spoke to me I used to blush and burst into tears.
DELMONTE. How sweet!
GEORGES. I'm honest and uncomplicated. (*He moves and stands between the chair* LC *and the piano*) I have deep faith in love and friendship. I'd willingly give my life for my friend Jacques, and he would give his for me. (*He moves up* C)
DELMONTE. Bravo! Bravo!
GEORGES. He's just opened the door to her. (*He moves down* C. *Feverishly*) I did my military services in the infantry at Tarbes. You used to send me parcels of gingerbread and chocolate every week.
MME DE MONTRACHET. Gingerbread and chocolates, right.
GEORGES. I studied engineering. I had chickenpox when I was a child.
MME DE MONTRACHET. All children have it.
GEORGES (*listening*) They're coming in now. There's no time to tell you any more. (*He sits on the sofa. Quickly*) I am very loyal, and a devoted son.

(*There is a pause as they wait, fixedly*)

(*Softly*) And I adore climbing trees.

(*The lights continue to fade as twilight falls.
The* BUTLER *enters hesitantly from the hall*)
BUTLER. Please, sir . . .

(GEORGES *sees the* BUTLER'S *embarrassment and stops* MME DE MONTRACHET *with a wave of his hand*)
GEORGES. What is it?
BUTLER (*moving* C) It's a hunchback, sir.
GEORGES. A hunchback?
BUTLER. Yes, sir. He says he's brought a message from Miss Barbara in Paris.
GEORGES (*leaping up*) Throw him out!
BUTLER (*with a gesture*) Oh! I couldn't, sir, a man afflicted like that. Anyway, he's gone already. He lives next door; he brought a telephone message for you, sir. (*He recites*) Miss Barbara in Paris couldn't find us in the directory, so she rang up number thirty-four, next door. Miss Barbara wants you to ring her as soon as possible, sir. It seems there has been some rumpus regarding you can guess what, so the lady said, sir—and if you do not show some sign of life immediately, there will be—I repeat Miss Barbara's own words, sir—there will be an awful bloody shindy.

(GEORGES *does not move; his fists are clenched*)

(*Impassively*) She said, "An awful bl———"
GEORGES. Yes—I heard you the first time—I shall have to go.

(GEORGES *exits brusquely to the hall and re-enters almost immediately, with his raincoat*)
If the young lady arrives while I'm away, make her welcome. If I'm not back in half an hour, it means I've had to go to Paris. So start dinner, don't wait for me.

(GEORGES *exits to the hall, before* DELMONTE *and* MME DE MONTRACHET *can make a move. They turn to the Butler*)
BUTLER (*oracularly*) An awful bloody shindy!

(*The* BUTLER *makes a gesture and exits to the hall, closing the door behind him. The* ACTORS *exchange a wan smile*)

DELMONTE (*rising*) I'm beginning to wonder, darling, if we oughtn't to have asked for payment in advance. (*He paces down* R *and whistles softly. He wants to appear indifferent*) Funny business, though, isn't it?
MME DE MONTRACHET. Oh, on the stage you come up with all sorts.
DELMONTE (*crossing to* R *of the chair* LC) Why's he putting on all this show for the girl? To seduce her? Kidnap her? Who knows? To . . . (*He makes a throat-cutting gesture*)

MME DE MONTRACHET (*leaping to her feet; with a little cry*) Oh, please! No. Don't talk such nonsense.

DELMONTE. Oh, you never know these days. (*He crosses to* R *of her*) When the butler announced that telephone call just now he gave me a wink.

MME DE MONTRACHET. A wink?

DELMONTE. Yes, a wink. Did Guillotard seem to know this young man well when he told you about him?

MME DE MONTRACHET. I gathered it was the first time he'd ever seen him.

DELMONTE. Ah! Ah! (*He crosses to the window*) It's quite dark already. A nice thing if we have to go out and look for help in this mass of little streets.

MME DE MONTRACHET (*suddenly*) Let's phone. (*She moves to the table up* C)

DELMONTE. Who to?

MME DE MONTRACHET. I don't know. Let's phone anybody. (*She lifts the telephone receiver. Into the telephone*) Hello? (*She pauses*) Oh!

DELMONTE (*furious because he is frightened*) What the devil's the matter? (*He moves to her*)

MME DE MONTRACHET. It's cut off.

(DELMONTE *seizes the receiver*)

DELMONTE (*into the telephone*) Hallo, hallo. (*He listens, then replaces the receiver, trembling*) Well, there's nothing extraordinary about that. Perhaps the line's out of order.

(MME DE MONTRACHET, *speechless, shows Delmonte the secret door down* R *which is opening of its own accord, as in a thriller. They instinctively draw together.*

The BUTLER *enters by the secret door down* R, *pushing it open with his foot. He carries a tray with two glasses of sherry*)

BUTLER (*moving to* R *of the sofa*) May I be allowed to serve some sherry to the lady and gentleman while they are waiting?

MME DE MONTRACHET (*in a faint voice*) You may be allowed —yes.

(*The* BUTLER *crosses to* MME DE MONTRACHET *and* DELMONTE *and they each take a glass of sherry, without taking their eyes off the* BUTLER, *who obviously has no intention of going out. He moves to the windows and closes the shutters. The room becomes dim except for lighted areas around the hall doors and to* R *of the piano*)

(*She murmurs, with a sign*) He is closing the shutters.

DELMONTE. You mustn't drink the sherry. I don't like the fellow's face.

(MME DE MONTRACHET, *who does not hear Delmonte, empties her glass*)

Mme de Montrachet. What did you say?
Delmonte (*seeing that she has drunk it; annoyed*) It doesn't matter now, my poor sweet. (*He moves to the piano*)
Butler (*crossing to Delmonte; confidentially*) Sir . . .
Delmonte (*startled; shouting*) What do you want?
Butler (*mysteriously*) Sh!
Delmonte (*stepping back and shouting*) What do you mean, "Sh"? Why—"Sh"?
Butler. I beg your pardon, sir, but do you know the house well, sir?
Delmonte. No—but—what about you?
Butler. I am hired, from Dufort's. (*He moves towards the hall doors*)

(Delmonte *follows the* Butler)

I was sent after the young man telephoned for a meal and servants at six o'clock. I only know this room, the dining-room, and the kitchen. That's why I asked you, sir. The house *seems* deserted. The young man said it was, anyway. Yet I can hear something pattering about—(*he points to the ceiling*) up there.
Delmonte (*filled with horror at this detail*) Pattering about?
Butler. Pattering about. Like a big mouse.
Delmonte (*repeating*) A big mouse?

(*The* Proprietress *enters from the hall. Her hair is in curling papers and she wears a nightgown and a white shawl.* Mme de Montrachet *and the* Butler *leap* R. Delmonte *staggers backwards, ending up on the piano stool*)

Proprietress. Oh! I'm sorry. I couldn't hear any more noise —I was getting worried. So sorry. Do forgive me.

(*The* Proprietress *exits discreetly to the hall. The others look questioningly at one another and move towards the hall doors*)

Butler. Did you see that old lady, sir, when you arrived?
Delmonte. No, did you?
Butler. No.

(*The front door bell rings*)

Mme de Montrachet (*with a cry*) Oh! Someone's ringing at the door.

(*There is a silence as they listen. The bell rings again*)

Butler (*in sepulchral tones*) Another ring.
Mme de Montrachet. Don't let's open it.
Delmonte. Still, we can't spend the night shut in here. See if you can see who it is through the window without showing yourself.

(*The* Butler *moves to the windows, opens the shutters a little, peers out, then returns to* c)

BUTLER. It's a young girl in a flowered dress and a white straw hat.

DELMONTE (*after a moment's hesitation; with a gesture of cold resolution*) Show her in.

The BUTLER *hesitates, then exits reluctantly to the hall.* DELMONTE *hurriedly drinks his sherry, puts his glass on the piano, picks up his newspapers and sits in the chair* LC. MME DE MONTRACHET *goes to the piano, sits and plays. They both prepare a bold front for the enemy as—*

the CURTAIN *falls*

ACT II

Scene i

Scene—*The linen-room in Christine's house in Paris. Five minutes later. The room is in the basement of the house of Christine Delachaume, Georges' wife. There are doors* R *and* L. *Built-in linen cupboards and a built-in ironing-board line the walls. A large ottoman or linen-chest is up* C *and there are laundry baskets down* R *and down* L. *There is a wooden chair up* R *and a stool* L. *A wall-telephone is fixed to the wall* R.

(*See the Ground Plan of the Scene*)

When the Curtain *rises,* Barbara, *a young woman, is speaking on the telephone. She is in evening dress.*

Barbara (*into the telephone*) Yes, yes, Georges, a dreadful scene. This time I'm convinced she's going to insist on a divorce. So if you're not doing anything really important, you might do worse than come home . . . I know it's not my business . . . No, I'm speaking from the linen-room; no-one ever comes in here . . . Of course not, I won't say a word . . . You are silly, darling . . . Do just as you please . . . Good night, Georges. Have a good time. (*She replaces the receiver and moves thoughtfully* C)

(Jacques *enters quickly* L. *He wears a dinner jacket*)

Jacques. Barbara! I thought you'd gone out. What have you been doing here for the last hour?
Barbara. Nothing, Jacques.
Jacques (*looking first at Barbara, then at the telephone*) I know that little dodge, telephoning from the linen-room. I thought of it before you did, my pet.
Barbara. Did you, Jacques?
Jacques. Who were you ringing?
Barbara (*looking him full in the face*) Who did you want me to ring?

(Jacques *hesitates, and blinks a little under her gaze*)

Jacques. Nobody's heard anything of him?
Barbara (*shortly*) Nobody. Not even me.
Jacques. If he isn't back before midnight, we're sunk.
Barbara (*archly*) A fine respectable family—not to mention friends—all thrown out on the street.
Jacques. Just what are you trying to insinuate, sweetie? We are guests here. The hosts are our closest friends. I should hate

to see them quarrel. It would be a double disappointment to me—first as their friend, and again, as their guest.

BARBARA (*sitting on the chair up* R) Guest—for two years?

JACQUES. We came to Georges' when we had to move out of our own house. In the first place it was for a fortnight. We were invited.

BARBARA. Yes, twenty-two months ago.

JACQUES (*with crashing complacency*) We haven't been able to find a flat. After all, is Georges my best friend, or isn't he? If a man can't stay at his best friend's any more, where is he going to stay? With strangers?

BARBARA. That's what people are usually reduced to.

JACQUES. Well, that's just the sort of thing I can't stand. I've always believed in friendship, and always shall.

BARBARA. Yes, Jacques.

JACQUES. He's only done what I'd have done, if I'd married a rich wife like he has, instead of being silly enough to marry you. I'd have said the same as he said to me: "You're hard up, Jacques, old chap, so make yourself at home here on me, act as my secretary, I'll give you sixty thousand francs a month for your pocket money."

BARBARA. He said thirty thousand.

JACQUES. That's right, but *I'd* have said sixty. That's what comes of having a generous nature. (*He sits on the ottoman*) I think it's nice down here, it was a very good idea of yours—it's private, and it's quiet. In the rest of the house, people are slamming doors and moaning in corners all over the place. They keep bombarding you with questions and waving revolvers in your face. Melodrama stuff! Huh!

(M. DELACHAUME *enters* L. *He is hearty and well-groomed, wearing tails and a monocle. He has an overcoat on his arm and carries a top hat*)

DELACHAUME. Oh! There you are. I've been looking for you both everywhere. (*He crosses to the doorway* R) These quarrels wear my nerves to shreds. I'm going to slip out by the side door and smoke a cigar in the open. She's got her eyes glued to the front door all the time. Still no news of the blighter?

JACQUES. None.

DELACHAUME. Outlook's pretty black.

JACQUES. Very black.

DELACHAUME. Just as we finished dressing for the Opera, my wife shot off like a lunatic, she said she'd just had an idea. Have you any faith in her ideas?

JACQUES. No.

DELACHAUME. Neither have I.

(DELACHAUME *exits* R. *When he has gone,* JACQUES *moves along the seat, nearer to Barbara*)

Scene i   DINNER WITH THE FAMILY

JACQUES. All the same, it's a bit thick of your friend Georges to play a trick like this on us.
BARBARA. *Your* friend Georges.
JACQUES. *Our* friend Georges, if you like. You're sure he's *not* said anything to you?
BARBARA (*rising, crossing and looking in the mirror* L) Why should he tell me any more than you, my dear?
JACQUES. Men always confide more in a woman, it's common knowledge. (*He rises, crosses and stands behind her*) Besides, Georges is very fond of you. You go out a lot together.
BARBARA. Is that a complaint?
JACQUES. No. Simply a statement. (*He crosses to* RC) Listen, Barbara, my love, we're man and wife, I know, but that doesn't stop us being friends. I may be wrong, of course, but I rather suspect you know something.
BARBARA (*moving to the stool down* L *and sitting*) You are wrong.
JACQUES. You don't think he's done a bunk like two years ago, when he tried to join the Foreign Legion?
BARBARA. He's told me nothing.
JACQUES. Christine's having one attack of hysterics after another upstairs in her bedroom. And it's *our* fate that's being decided by all this, remember. (*He crosses to Barbara*) If Christine insists on a divorce and we're all flung into the street, it means back to the typing-pool for you, honey.
BARBARA. Well, then, back to the typing-pool it'll have to be, honey.
JACQUES (*looking at her; in all sincerity; bluntly*) You sicken me. That's all I can say. You make me sick!

(*The telephone rings.* BARBARA *rises and they both rush to the telephone. There is a short struggle.* JACQUES *holds the telephone receiver in one hand and Barbara with the other*)

Ah! So that's what you were waiting for, eh, old girl?
BARBARA. Jacques, let go. Let go, do you hear? I forbid you to answer it. Beast! Filthy beast!
JACQUES (*into the telephone*) Hello? . . . Who? Am I who? . . . No, of course I am not Esme. Who's speaking? . . . Eh? . . . What message? . . . The little fair chap from the hair-dresser's won't be able to go to the cinema this evening? . . . Right. I'll tell her. (*He releases Barbara and sheepishly replaces the receiver*)

(BARBARA *bursts out laughing, crosses and sits on the stool* L)

(*He looks resentfully at Barbara for a moment, then crosses to her*) Shut up, Barbara. Let's forget ourselves for the moment. If Christine gets a divorce do you think *Georges* is going to be happy? Can you see him going back to car-selling at fifty thousand francs a month, including expenses, after four years of luxury? (*He moves* C) It's all very well Georges getting on his high horse with Christine,

c

but if he hadn't married her and her money four years ago, where would he be today? He's got brilliant qualifications as a lounger and a scrounger, but nothing else. Where do you think a chronic loafer like that would be if he hadn't married well?

BARBARA. Where will you be tomorrow, if he can't keep you any longer?

JACQUES (*moving to Barbara and squatting beside her*) In queer street, like he is himself. You're not telling me anything, duckie. I know. That's why I'm humble. That's why I don't say anything, even when you go out with him a bit too often in the afternoon. 'Cos there's one thing you'll both have to learn—you two really taught me this—in this life nobody plays fast and loose with the people who provide the money. If you happen to earn your living in my lady Christine's arms, it's no good trying to be clever; your place is there, in my lady's arms and nowhere else. And you mustn't complain. (*Quietly*) I don't.

BARBARA (*quietly*) You revolt me, Jacques.

JACQUES. Yes. It's not very nice, I grant you—less for me than for you, in fact. After all, you can comfort yourself with the thought that you do all this because you love him—whereas I . . . (*He rises, moves to the mirror and combs his hair*) Oh, what the hell! (*He speaks to himself in the mirror and preens himself*) Jacques, you've got a sweet old mother in the country with a comfortable income. You endured a proper Catholic education with the priests. You learnt Latin. *Bellum, bellum, bellum, belli, bello, bello.* You're not just a lout. You want to remind yourself of that, now and again. (*He crosses to* C) Take Poppa Edgar outside, wallowing in his cigar; he'd be shocked to death if you told him he was living by sponging on his son.

(JACQUES *crosses to Barbara and offers her a cigarette.* BARBARA *takes a cigarette and* JACQUES *lights them both.*

DELACHAUME, *smoking a cigar, enters* R)

DELACHAUME. I'm getting bored out there. Ah! This is no sort of life for a man of my age. Tell me, what the devil are you two doing in the linen-room?

JACQUES. Getting a change of air.

DELACHAUME. Oh! Quite right. The atmosphere in this house is too thick to breathe. (*He is carried away*) Damn it, I'm not to blame if my son decides to spend the night away from home. (*He suddenly thinks of something else*) Do you think we shall go to the Opera?

JACQUES. The chances look mildly jeopardized to me.

DELACHAUME (*wandering down* R) And I was so looking forward to it. I adore *Faust*. (*He sings a few bars of the waltz, then stops with a sigh*) Ah, well! Still no news, of course?

JACQUES. Still no news.

DELACHAUME. I can't fathom that boy, playing the idiot like

Scene 1   DINNER WITH THE FAMILY   31

this. I mean—Christine's charming—a bit highly-strung, perhaps, and a bit jealous, but absolutely charming in spite of that. What's your opinion?
  JACQUES. Charming. Has anyone managed to relieve her of that little pearl-handled revolver?
  DELACHAUME. Esme has, I think—I hope—I don't know. In my time men used to deceive their wives, of course, but they went about it more skilfully. It was no more heinous a crime for that. What's your opinion?
  BARBARA. I haven't an opinion.
  DELACHAUME. Of course, I don't say this boy of mine is absolutely obliged to deceive Christine. Far be it from me to suggest such a thing. (*He moves to the chair up* R *and sits*) But what I can't understand about you young people is this taste for crudity you all have. You all say you like clear-cut situations. So we old people think: "Good. They're going to put themselves into clear-cut situations. They're going to teach us to behave." Nothing of the kind, nothing of the kind. You're men just the same as we are, and you get into exactly the same old situations, old as the world itself. Only you're different, oh, yes. You turn your behind squarely to the rest of the world and you think that makes the situation clear-cut. (*He rises. Furiously*) I prefer the old hypocrites by far. In the long run they did much less harm. What's your opinion?
  JACQUES (*to Barbara*) Your opinion?
  BARBARA (*shaking her head*) Haven't got one.
  JACQUES. She has none.
  DELACHAUME. When I was your age I was never short of opinions about anything. (*He moves down* R) I can't understand this youngster of mine. He has a lovely wife, madly in love with him, and she's rich. What more does he want? Answer me that.
  JACQUES. What more does he want? Answer him that.
  BARBARA. I wouldn't know.
  JACQUES. She wouldn't know.
  DELACHAUME. Nothing. There *is* nothing else. Money, love, you can't want anything else. Life's very simple after all, damn it. I don't understand you people. He says he's unhappy. Why is he unhappy? Take me. I'm an unsuccessful old artist—a failure, and I've had a hard life. But am I unhappy? Are you unhappy?
  JACQUES. Speaking for myself, I'm very happy.
  DELACHAUME (*to Barbara*) And you?
  JACQUES. And you, dear?
  BARBARA (*feelingly*) Divinely happy.
  DELACHAUME. Well, then? He says he doesn't love his wife. Neither did I love my wife. Did I make such a fuss, just because of that? He says we pushed him into it. Georges was earning fifty thousand francs a month as a car-salesman and he had three

million francs' worth of debts of honour still to settle for the family. He would never have finished paying them off. He meets a young girl in high society, ravishing to look at and madly in love with him—and she inherits a fortune. He flirts with her, everything's going fine. Then, suddenly, whoosh! The boy develops a conscience; he begins to have doubts about whether he should marry her or not. His mother and I, thank God, soon settled that for him. Don't you think we did the right thing? (*To Barbara*) What's your opinion?

JACQUES. She's certain not to have one.

(ESME, *Christine's maid, enters* L)

ESME. Ah, here you are.

JACQUES (*moving to Esme; ingratiatingly*) What's the news, Esme?

ESME. Oh, M. Jacques, if only you could see my arm. It's been like that since first thing this morning. She can't speak to me without digging her nails into my flesh. Oh, she's in such a state. Still no news of the master?

JACQUES. Still no news.

DELACHAUME (*moving down* R) He can't be long now, I'm quite sure. Quite sure.

ESME (*rubbing her arm*) Well, it's not for me to say, but I think the master should consider us a bit.

(*A bell suddenly rings*)

(*She shouts*) Coming, madame. (*To the others*) I can't leave her for a minute. M. Edgar, sir, would you ask cook for some camomile tea from the kitchen?

DELACHAUME (*adjusting his monocle*) Camomile tea.

(*The bell rings*)

ESME (*crossing to Delachaume*) Yes, please. But don't let Jeannette bring it up. (*She crosses to the door* L) She can't bear the sight of her. She'd scratch her eyes out.

DELACHAUME (*following Esme*) I'll bring it up myself.

ESME. On a tray, and don't forget the traycloth, please, M. Edgar. If you do, I'll be the one who's to blame.

DELACHAUME. On a tray, with a traycloth. It shall be done.

(ESME *exits* L. DELACHAUME *turns to go, then stops.*
MADAME DELACHAUME *sweeps in* R. *She is elegant and is youngly clothed in evening dress and cloak. She carries a man's hat*)

MME DELACHAUME. Oh, here you are. I've been looking everywhere for you. My darlings, I've got wonderful news for you.

JACQUES. Have you been to the police?

MME DELACHAUME (*crossing to* C) No, to Madame Lerida, the

SCENE 1   DINNER WITH THE FAMILY

clairvoyante. I took one of Georges' hats, and she swears he's not left the Paris area.

(JACQUES *takes the hat and looks at it*)

JACQUES. That's my hat, now. He gave it to me a month ago.

MME DELACHAUME. Oh, there. That muddles everything up. Then it must be you who has not left the Paris area. What a pity. I'll have to go back to Madame Lerida. She can tell us everything, she's frighteningly clairvoyante. Right at the start she told me how old I was. What's Christine feeling like?

JACQUES. She wants to die.

MME DELACHAUME. That's better! That proves she still loves him. We're not going to the Opera now, I suppose?

JACQUES. No need. We're in the middle of an opera here, prima-donna and all.

MME DELACHAUME. No opera, good. (*She sits on the ottoman*) One less bore to go through, thank God. *Oh!* I've got another piece of news. Very nasty this one. The cook told me that she had a visitor this afternoon—Dupont Dupres.

DELACHAUME. Her solicitor!

MME DELACHAUME. Yes.

DELACHAUME. That boy has done for us now. Oh, my God, that camomile tea.

(DELACHAUME *rushes out* R)

MME DELACHAUME. We must do something, we've got to do something. It's really ridiculous to let so much happiness crumble away like this, for no apparent reason. I mean ... Oh, I could slap Georges. I adore him, of course, he's my son, but I'd slap him like a baby, if I had hold of him.

JACQUES. Yes, that's just it. You can hardly slap him if you haven't got hold of him. Where is he?

MME DELACHAUME. I can't give up living in this house. I'd rather die. I'd kill myself. Some people just can't breathe outside an atmosphere of luxury. (*She rises*) Take away their luxury and they die. (*She suddenly notices her reflection in the mirror*) What do you think of my little hat?

JACQUES (*coldly polite*) Revolutionary.

MME DELACHAUME. Christine gave it to me. She'd only worn it once. It cost twenty thousand francs, this hat.

(ESME *enters* L, *crosses and stands in front of the ottoman, looking serious. They all turn to her*)

ESME. It's all up this time.

MME DELACHAUME. What's all up? (*She moves to* L *of Esme*) You frighten me, Esme, my dear.

ESME (*weighing her words*) Madame's leaving him.

MME DELACHAUME (*with a shriek*) Esme, it can't be true.

Esme. True as I'm standing here.

(Delachaume *enters triumphantly* r. *He carries a tray with a cup of camomile tea*)

Delachaume. Here's the camomile tea, with traycloth.

Esme. Madame won't want it now. She's getting up. She says it's stupid wasting her life away like this, for nothing. Well, it's no more than he deserves.

Mme Delachaume. Esme, you surely can't think such a thing.

Esme. Oh, yes, I can. I'm a woman, and I can see myself in her position. Besides we all need a bit of peace and quiet in this house.

Mme Delachaume. Esme, my dear Esme, you have a heart of gold. You can't do this to us.

Esme. I kept advising madame, as long as I could, to be patient. Now, it's more than my job's worth. I have to agree with her, now.

Mme Delachaume (*crossing to Delachaume*) Oh, no, she can't do that. It's too silly, when all's said and done. I may be Georges' mother, but I am also Christine's friend. (*She crosses to the doorway* l) I'll go and speak to her.

Esme (*shouting*) She's locked herself in her room. She won't answer you.

Mme Delachaume. We'll soon see. The poor child always adored me.

(Mme Delachaume *exits* l)

Esme (*to the others*) As long as she adored the master, perhaps —but not now. (*She crosses to Delachaume*) Don't fool yourselves about it. If it's all over with the master, there's very little hope left for the family. What do you expect? It's all very well, you keep on and on loving someone, but if that person doesn't love you in return, you know, sooner or later . . .

Delachaume (*furiously*) But, by God—why the devil doesn't he love her?

(Mme Delachaume *enters* l)

Mme Delachaume (*moving to* l *of Esme; annoyed*) She won't see me, she's locked her door.

Esme. What did I tell you? If the master doesn't come home tonight, madame's going away tomorrow morning and everybody will have to clear out.

Mme Delachaume. What, in one day?

Esme. Madame said that when she wasn't here, no-one else was to remain in the house.

Delachaume. Good Lord, it's crazy! Why, even servants get a week's notice.

Scene 1   DINNER WITH THE FAMILY   35

Esme. But you're not a servant, are you, sir? Servants are workers, and have trade unions. It's not the same thing.

(Delachaume *stiffens, quite beside himself, and brings his monocle into action*)

Delachaume. This girl's insolence is too much. Who exactly do you think you're dealing with? Let me tell you, we are people with some standing, only I see we made the mistake of allowing you too much freedom and familiarity.

Esme. "Standing", did you say? Hm! You make me laugh. You're only a bunch of phoneys.

Delachaume (*tranquilly*) I don't know what she means. I never did understand slang.

Mme Delachaume. Esme. My dear Esme. You must be patient and excuse M. Edgar. You know how eccentric he is, he's an artist, you see.

(Esme *turns and crosses towards the doorway* l, *stopping up* c)

Esme, listen to me—what if we were to promise you something for using your influence.

Esme. Nothing doing. Sorry. I think you and the master are out of luck from now on. In any case, what you could manage to scrape up between you . . .

(Esme *exits* l. Mme Delachaume *sits on the ottoman*. Delachaume *sits on the chair up* r)

Mme Delachaume. This time we're finished, destitute. My courage will never hold out. I am too old to—er—I mean, I'm too young. I'm too young to resign myself to it.

Jacques. Ah! Our precious Georges, who can't bear wearing a tie more than three times. Too fastidious, he likes ringing the changes. Now, he'll have to keep putting them on till they look like bits of string.

Barbara. I know it's only a detail, Jacques, but that means you'll have to start buying some yourself.

Jacques. I don't care a damn! I'd be glad never to wear a collar and tie again and have holes in the seats of my pants, for the pleasure of seeing him on his beam ends.

Barbara (*leaping up and crossing to Jacques*) Shut up, you're nauseating.

Jacques. You don't know what it's like to grow up with somebody who's handsomer than you are, who was always brighter at school and then gets rich into the bargain. That's what's so attractive about revolutions, I always think—even if you don't care a damn about the principles, it must be wonderful watching people who've always been carefree and confident suddenly plunged into misery, croaking their last.

(Barbara *crosses to the doorway* r)

And Georges'll croak, all right, he's such a sensitive chap—he'll just give up the ghost, I know him.

DELACHAUME (*prostrate*) If only we knew where he was. We could at least warn him that tonight is his last chance. Absolutely the last.

(JACQUES *crosses to* BARBARA)

JACQUES (*softly; in a hoarse voice*) Maybe we'll all croak, but he'll be the first to go.

BARBARA (*suddenly bursting out*) I can't bear this. I followed him the other day. He's rented a house—thirty-two rue Victor at Senlis. I suppose that's where he must be.

JACQUES. Hell! Why didn't you say so before, damn your eyes? I've got the car outside. Quick, all of you.

JACQUES *drags* MME DELACHAUME *by the hand, pushes* DELACHAUME *off* L *and follows with* MME DELACHAUME. BARBARA *quickly follows them off as—*

the CURTAIN *falls*

SCENE 2

SCENE—*The drawing-room at Senlis. About an hour later.*

When the CURTAIN *rises, the lights are on.* ISABELLE, *a young girl dressed in white, is standing* C. *The* PROPRIETRESS *and the* BUTLER *are sitting on the sofa.* DELMONTE *is seated in the armchair* LC. MME DE MONTRACHET *is seated at the piano.*

ISABELLE. Are you quite sure he didn't even know you an hour ago?

DELMONTE. Are we sure! Why, we arrived on the seven-ten and came straight here. We'd never set eyes on him before.

ISABELLE. And he's really rented this house for a month?

PROPRIETRESS. I don't normally let by the month, of course, but he seemed such a nice young man, the sort you'd trust without question—you know.

ISABELLE. Yes, you would, wouldn't you? (*She sighs a little and turns to the Butler*) And you were going to play the old and faithful servant?

BUTLER. Yes, miss.

ISABELLE (*looking at him; pleasantly*) Isn't that dreadful.

BUTLER. Oh, I was in a very wealthy household for seventeen years, miss. Only now I work for Dufort's—I simply came in answer to a telephone call. We were asked for a Number Two type menu for four people.

ISABELLE. Four people? Why four? There would have been five, with Jacques.

BUTLER. Now you've broken the crust, you may as well taste

the fruit, miss. The fifth person wasn't going to have anything to eat, miss.
MME DE MONTRACHET (*clucking*) That was the friend.
DELMONTE. The best friend in the world. Ha, ha!
ISABELLE. Jacques?
DELMONTE. That's right. Jacques. The wonderful Jacques.
ISABELLE (*moving to Delmonte*) Jacques wasn't having anything to eat? Why not?
DELMONTE. For a very good reason . . .
MME DE MONTRACHET (*with a guffaw*) He's got no stomach for it. He doesn't exist.
ISABELLE (*moving to R of the piano*) Jacques doesn't exist?
DELMONTE. No more than we do. (*Hopefully*) But we can eat, at least—can't we, Emilienne?
MME DE MONTRACHET. Any time it's convenient.
ISABELLE. No, that's not true. Jacques does exist, I'm sure of it. We've talked about him every day for the last two months.
DELMONTE. Pure imagination, all of it.
ISABELLE. But I've seen his photograph.
DELMONTE. A fake! Nothing would surprise me, where that spry young man's concerned.
ISABELLE (*wandering to the window; softly*) There's nothing left at all, then, if even Jacques is a lie? (*She places her bag and gloves on the window-seat*)
DELMONTE. He's Jack-in-the-box, that's who he is. Here one minute and gone the next. (*He laughs*)
MME DE MONTRACHET. He said he was going to make a telephone call. It may have been a trick to leave us and get away.
DELMONTE (*with a guffaw*) Oh, this is absolutely priceless. (*He stops, then repeats thoughtfully*) Priceless. (*He rises. Suddenly angry*) Yes, that reminds me—if he doesn't come back, who's going to pay us? (*He crosses to the piano*)
MME DE MONTRACHET (*rising*) I had a sort of feeling there was something fishy about the whole business.
DELMONTE. Just a minute, just a minute. I'm a Union man, I'll soon have them on to him. He won't get away with a trick like that, with me.
MME DE MONTRACHET. What are you going to do, then, Mr Know-all? You don't even know his address.
DELMONTE. Guillotard knows it.
MME DE MONTRACHET. That's what you think. He told me the young man had given *this* address.
PROPRIETRESS (*anxiously*) Tell me, they can't impound my furniture and hold me responsible, can they?
DELMONTE. I have no idea, madame. I know nothing about it. You should take advice on these matters when you let to strangers.
PROPRIETRESS. How was I to know? He seemed to me quite genuine, a young man of good education, good family, and so on.

DELMONTE (*jeering*) Good family, ha, ha! Let me laugh at that one. (*He crosses to* C) That was us. We're his family. Ha! You've got a funny idea of families, I must say.

MME DE MONTRACHET. Oh, dear, oh, dear, there's one born every minute.

DELMONTE. He's a very slippery customer, this fellow. Ha! Young man of very good family. It hits you in the eye, really. (*He crosses to Isabelle*) As for you, young lady, I'm quite ready to believe you've been taken in, so were we—but if you were my daughter, I'd see you found something out about young men before you had much to do with them. (*He moves* C)

ISABELLE (*moving to* R *of Delmonte*) I won't let you speak like that. How much were you supposed to get if this plan had come off this evening, as it was meant to?

MME de MONTRACHET (*crossing to Delmonte; hastily*) Four thousand francs, that's the rate for outside Paris.

DELMONTE (*quite as eagerly*) Plus travelling expenses, of course. Travelling is never included in the fee.

(ISABELLE *goes to her handbag, takes some notes from it and returns to Delmonte*)

ISABELLE. Here are—ten thousand francs.

DELMONTE. It's a bit much, don't you think, your being drawn into a pantomime like this and then having to pay the actors into the bargain? (*He takes the notes*) All right, it's your business. I'll give you the change. (*He feels in his pockets*)

(MME DE MONTRACHET *wanders to the piano*)

Er—have you got any change, darling? (*He moves to Mme de Montrachet*)

MME DE MONTRACHET. Er—I don't know, how much do you want?

ISABELLE. Please, don't bother. It's a small bonus for playing your part so well.

(DELMONTE *looks sour and stiffly pockets the money*)

(*She moves to* R *of the chair* LC) Do you usually play in straight plays or musicals?

DELMONTE. I play everything, classical and modern plays, tragedies and comedies.

ISABELLE. And you never get them muddled, mix them up at all?

DELMONTE. Never used to in the old days. Comedy was comedy, and tragedy was tragedy. But with the plays we get served up now-a-days, of course . . .

ISABELLE. When you've been cast to play a good and noble father, do you usually welcome the heroine in the way you welcomed me?

Scene 2 DINNER WITH THE FAMILY 39

DELMONTE. Oh, now, that's going a bit too far. You're not going to complain at my telling you the truth, I hope? You were being hoaxed, my dear girl, diddled, swindled, spoofed.
ISABELLE. Perhaps I was, but you were being paid to swindle me, and after all, it's your profession.
DELMONTE. Wait a minute. Let's have no aspersions on the stage, please. Don't you understand, I stepped out of character simply because I felt some villainy was afoot? Do you think I'm the sort to turn accomplice to a briber and corrupter? Or a petty thief who may only have been after your handbag?
ISABELLE. If that's what he wants, poor boy, there's very little left for him now. (*She moves to the Butler*) What do I owe you?
BUTLER (*rising*) Six thousand, eight hundred. (*He takes a bill from his pocket*) Hm! (*He has second thoughts*) Er—that is to say, just one moment, miss. (*He resumes his seat on the sofa, takes a pencil from his pocket, sucks it and studies the bill*)
MME DE MONTRACHET. You know, really, as woman to woman, I think he's treated you very badly.
DELMONTE (*sitting in the chair* LC) Shamefully. Young scamp. If I'd got him there I'd pull his ears straight out of his head.
ISABELLE (*gently*) Poor Georges. He'd thought up such a wonderful story. And when he comes back he'll find his worthy parents in a state of revolt and the old and faithful servant busy cooking the accounts.
BUTLER (*rising*) What's that? Pardon me—but I—was—er—I was checking the figures.
ISABELLE (*smiling*) Well, how much does it come to, now you've checked the figures?
BUTLER (*coughing to give himself confidence*) Hmm—eight thousand, one hundred and sixty—I'd forgotten the extras.
ISABELLE (*smiling*) All right. (*She hands the Butler some notes*) Hurry up and take your money, then you can all three go. You've nothing to keep you here, now.
DELMONTE. Right! (*He rises, stands below the piano, strikes an attitude and quotes theatrically*) "Farewell! Farewell! God knows when we shall meet again—or who has justice on his side!"
ISABELLE. I'm sure it must be you—but please hurry. When Georges returns I don't think he'll be in the mood to congratulate you.
DELMONTE. That's true. (*He moves towards the hall. To the Proprietress*) What time's the next train to Paris, Lady Macbeth?
PROPRIETRESS (*rising*) Hm! (*Coldly*) At this time of night I'm afraid there are no more trains at all. But if you all care to come to the kitchen, we will look it up in the time-table.

(*The* BUTLER, *the* PROPRIETRESS, DELMONTE *and* MME DE MONTRACHET *exit to the hall.* ISABELLE *wanders dreamily and regretfully around the room, finishing* R *of the piano*)

ISABELLE. All the grandmothers are part of the trick. The old servant, the house, even the furniture—none of it is real. What a pity.

(JACQUES *enters warily from the hall, like someone entering a room unannounced in a strange house. He notices Isabelle and stops*)

JACQUES. Excuse me, but all the doors were open and anyone can walk in—it's like a shop. (*He moves down* C) I would like to speak to M. Georges Delachaume.

ISABELLE (*looking at Jacques for a moment; suddenly crying out*) Good evening, Jacques.

JACQUES (*stopping in his tracks*) Good God! Who told you my name?

ISABELLE. I guessed it.

JACQUES (*not in the least upset*) Oh! Clairvoyante? Where's your crystal?

ISABELLE (*crossing to him*) Wait a minute. Are you an actor? You can speak quite freely, I know all about it.

(JACQUES *is rather amazed*)

JACQUES (*after a moment of painful reflection*) Excuse me, but this house is Number thirty-two, isn't it?

ISABELLE. Yes.

JACQUES. Rue Victor?

ISABELLE. Yes, yes.

JACQUES (*beginning an explanation*) You see, I'm a friend of M. Georges Delachaume . . .

ISABELLE. Yes—his childhood friend, in fact. Your name is Jacques Lebos. You are twenty-six. You've come here this evening to have dinner with me.

JACQUES. Oh, no! That last bit was wrong. I've just had a meal, thank you. But it doesn't matter, don't let that put you off.

(ISABELLE *walks slowly around Jacques, finishing* R *of him*)

Even the best clairvoyantes make a mistake now and then. Do go on. This is most interesting.

ISABELLE (*looking at him all the time*) Stand up straight, first.

JACQUES. What?

ISABELLE. Look me in the eyes.

JACQUES. Well . . .?

ISABELLE (*gravely*) You're standing straight, aren't you?

JACQUES. Yes—why?

ISABELLE. How is it you're not taller than that?

JACQUES (*a bit put out by this conversation*) I can't really say. I'm doing as well as I can.

ISABELLE. Georges told me you were as tall as he is.

JACQUES. Has Georges been talking about me?

ISABELLE. Of course he has. Georges hardly ever talks of anything else. Does that surprise you?

Scene 2   DINNER WITH THE FAMILY   41

JACQUES. A little, yes. Er—do you think I could hear what my friend Georges has been saying about me?
ISABELLE (*smiling*) A lot of awful things, of course.
JACQUES. Oh! Of course. But—er—anything else?
(ISABELLE *looks at Jacques in silence for a few moments*)
ISABELLE. No—I'm sure you're not an actor, you would have been straightening your tie, then, just to try to look natural.
(JACQUES, *in spite of himself, straightens his tie.*
The BUTLER *enters from the hall and moves between Isabelle and Jacques*)
BUTLER. Excuse me, miss, but would it be possible, do you think, now, for me to announce dinner? It is after ten o'clock. It would fall in with the wishes of those other persons—(*with a look of mistrust towards Jacques*) you know of. The persons—(*with another look at Jacques*) that—er—you know of, miss, are as a matter of fact obliged to spend the night in the kitchen. There is no train for Paris until tomorrow morning.
ISABELLE. How late do Dufort's guarantee to serve their meals?
BUTLER. Midnight, miss.
ISABELLE. Well, we'll wait till midnight.
BUTLER (*with a gesture*) As you please, miss. However, there is no refrigerator in the kitchen, so I must warn you now, miss, that I can't be held responsible till midnight for the taste of the fish sauce.
(*The* BUTLER *goes into the hall and exits to* R)
JACQUES. What does all that mean?
ISABELLE. Believe it or not I was counting on you to explain.
JACQUES. On me? Tell me, where are we exactly?
ISABELLE. In a furnished house rented by Georges, so that he could have me to dinner this evening.
JACQUES (*moving to the hall doors*) A four-storeyed house! At Senlis, too, of all places.
ISABELLE (*moving to him*) You see, he meant it to be the house where he was born.
JACQUES. Where he was born? I like that!
(*They move down* C)
And that undertaker's assistant who just went out?
ISABELLE. That's a butler from Dufort's. He was to play the old family servant.
JACQUES. Well, well, well!
ISABELLE (*crossing to* R *of the sofa*) In the kitchen there are two actors, hired. They were to be his mother and father.
JACQUES. Marvellous! And you? What was your part in all this? By the way, who are you?

ISABELLE. I'm one of his girl-friends.
JACQUES. Oh, yes. Georges has never been short of them. A girl-friend from where?
ISABELLE. Nowhere in particular. That may distinguish me from the others, I hope. I met him in the Louvre, by the Egyptian mummies.
JACQUES. Mummies! Ho! Wonderful! That's the company he keeps now-a-days, is it? He would find something different. (*He moves to the piano and leans on it*) He drops us all in the cart so that he can go gallivanting round museums. Well, well, well!
ISABELLE (*after a pause*) I wonder why he didn't want us two to meet.
JACQUES. I wonder, too. (*He pauses*) Do you know what time he's coming back?
ISABELLE. He'd left when I arrived; there was no message.
JACQUES (*sitting in the chair* LC) Charming evening.
ISABELLE (*looking at him*) It's funny, you know. He swears that he tells you everything that happens to him, and yet he's never spoken to you about me?
JACQUES. He must have forgotten.
ISABELLE (*crossing to* R *of him*) You *are* his friend, though, aren't you?
JACQUES. His life-long friend, don't doubt that for a moment. His only real, intimate friend. As close as could be—we are what you might call Siamese friends.
ISABELLE (*after a pause*) Is it true that you saved his life once, when he fell out of a boat into the sea?
JACQUES. No, I'm afraid not—I can't swim.
ISABELLE (*after a moment's silence*) Oh! And the girl you were both in love with when you were eighteen, the girl you sacrificed to him?
JACQUES. Me, sacrifice a girl? I don't remember that.
ISABELLE (*moving up* C *and turning*) Oh, I must find something that's true. Didn't you sell all your furniture one day just so that Georges could buy a new shirt, and some decent clothes? Didn't you?
JACQUES (*with a guffaw*) Did he say I sold my furniture?
(ISABELLE *moves to* R *of Jacques*)
No. My God, that fellow's imagination. It's like the Arabian Nights when he can get a woman to listen to him. Sold my furniture! That's the latest. I'll give him sacrifice and devotion. He invents a wonderful devoted friend to dazzle the ladies, and then he has the cheek to call him by my name. (*He rises*) Well, let me tell you what we really are, your precious Georges and I . . .
ISABELLE (*moving to the window*) No! No, I don't want to hear.
JACQUES (*following Isabelle*) Don't you really? That'd be much too easy.

ISABELLE. *He* must tell me, then, not you.
JACQUES. Oh, no, I will. He told you I loved him and he loved me like a brother? Well, the truth is, Georges hates me, and I hate Georges like poison. We're life-long friends, that's true enough, and our nurses walked us out together, we were almost suckled together. But hatred came to us with the age of discretion, and since then, believe me, we've made up for lost time.
ISABELLE. Well, what are you doing with him day after day? Why are you here this evening?
JACQUES. I cling to him, little lady, as the shell clings to the rocks, and for the only reason that makes people really inseparable: self-interest—he keeps me.
ISABELLE. But why does *he* want you near him?
JACQUES. He needs me every day, so that he can humiliate me, so that he can send me on errands for him. Or rather, I should say, he needs my wife.
ISABELLE. Your wife?
JACQUES (*bowing graciously*) Just as I have the honour to inform you, with shame on my brow. He needs my wife. You don't seem to understand me properly. Yet I'm speaking as clearly as I can. Need I be more explicit, my choice of words more picturesque?
ISABELLE (*moving above the sofa*) Be quiet! You're disgusting.
JACQUES (*moving to* R *of Isabelle*) That's my speciality—I always disgust people. Someone else told me that only a moment ago. Whereas everything about M. Georges has style, and style is so important, isn't it? No hint of anything common about *him*. Take these actors he's hired to play his father and mother—the noble parents, ha! And this venerable old house. I'll bet he just loves it all. His friend, too—me—done with a flourish in the grand manner—nothing by halves, no, all M. Georges' dreams are on a grand scale. But they are *dreams*. This is a dream. Why, if he really had a friend like that, a man of flesh and blood, he'd have to pay heavily in hard cash for his noble, unselfish devotion.

(*The* BUTLER *enters distractedly from the hall*)

BUTLER. Miss—miss, some more persons. I don't know what to do. I'm swamped.

(DELACHAUME, MME DELACHAUME *and* BARBARA *enter from the hall*.
The BUTLER *goes into the hall and exits to* L)

DELACHAUME. Well, Jacques, in God's name . . .
MME DELACHAUME. We were getting worried, it's nearly eleven o'clock.
JACQUES. Ah! You've come just at the right time. The atmosphere is most propitious. The very moment for a dramatic entrance. Right in the purple passage. Come on! Gather round.

(DELACHAUME *and* MME DELACHAUME *move* C. BARBARA *stands by the piano*)

Do you know what this young lady has just told me—this charming person waiting here for M. Georges, with tears in her eyes and hand on her heart? Georges loves me, and I love him.

DELACHAUME (*understanding nothing*) My God! What a welcome! Tell me, who is the young lady?

JACQUES. Aha! She's Maria Marten in person, the mystery girl from a woman's weekly. The pale and delicate heroine, trembling and afraid, who is dragged by M. Georges through dark and terrible adventures.

DELACHAUME (*deciding to take no notice of Jacques' talk*) Where are we, anyway?

JACQUES. In the Chinaman's house. The villain's. The doors open of their own accord, the lotus plants are telephones, and the telephones are lotuses. Look at these tapestries, these green plants and bowls, these family portraits. They're all fishy. Very, very, fishy. Careful, Edgar, careful. Look beneath your feet, that little fault in the carpet there. That's the trap door.

(DELACHAUME *leaps backwards*)

That's their entrance. That's the way they'll come in.

DELACHAUME. Who, *who*, in God's name? I don't understand a word you're saying. *Who* will come in?

JACQUES. *They* will. The others. The Chinaman's guests.

(DELMONTE *and* MME DE MONTRACHET *enter from the hall*)

(*He stamps with joy*) Look! What did I say? Here they are.

(DELMONTE *and* MME DE MONTRACHET *are bewildered and exit in the hall to* L)

(*He moves to the window-seat and stands on it*) Ladies and Gentlemen! This house is a complete fake. It's stuffed with Mummies and Daddies. Lift up that armchair, you're sure to find a Gran'ma underneath, and a best friend in every drawer. All of it invented piece by piece to dazzle an innocent girl. (*He falls off the window-seat and leans on the back of the sofa*) Ah, no, I shall die of it, I shall bust before the night's out. (*It is impossible to tell whether he is laughing or crying. He shouts at Barbara*) Did you hear that? (*He crosses to Barbara*) It beats anything.

(ISABELLE *moves to* R *of the sofa*)

M. Georges invented a family. But that's nothing unusual, people do it every day. *He* had to go one better than that. *He* told her that I loved him and that he loved me. Do you hear? Don't you want to laugh? He loves me, he said. Don't you want to split your sides?

Scene 2 — DINNER WITH THE FAMILY

BARBARA (*looking at Isabelle all the time; gently*) Shut up, Jacques.
JACQUES. What did you say?
BARBARA. I'm just telling you it's time you shut up.
JACQUES. Shut up? Don't you see that now things have gone as far as this, we can't shut up any longer? (*He crosses to Mme Delachaume and pushes her over to face Isabelle*) Mme Delachaume, speak out. Now's the time, if ever. Put your hand on your heart, strike an attitude and quick about it. (*He moves to Delachaume and propels him to* L *of Mme Delachaume*) Edgar, come on, make your moustaches tremble, be noble and dignified as never before—this is the moment. Tell her you must have your son back immediately, that the family's whole future is at stake. (*He gives Delachaume a final push, then crosses and stands above the chair* LC) Come on, what are you waiting for? This is your big scene.
MME DELACHAUME (*very much "the mother" when she begins*) My dear—I realize, of course, that all this must be very distressing for you, as it is for us, but I am speaking to you now as a mother. You appear to be a respectable young girl—you'll understand me, I'm sure. My son has been telling you a pack of lies. You must send him back to us.
DELACHAUME (*thinking this is all true*) The boy is on the verge of breaking up his home, young lady.
MME DELACHAUME. You hold our happiness—the happiness of all of us here—in your hands. Let me explain . . .
ISABELLE (*stiffening*) No.
MME DELACHAUME. What do you mean—"no"?
ISABELLE. I don't want any explanation.
DELACHAUME. Well, if that isn't the most ridiculous . . . Now, listen to me . . .
ISABELLE (*moving to the window and collecting her belongings*) I'll stop my ears up, I won't listen. I'll wait for Georges in the next street, if need be, but I will not listen to your explanations.
MME DELACHAUME. You're being childish. You've got to hear the whole story sooner or later.
ISABELLE (*throwing her belongings back on the window-seat*) From Georges, but not from you.
DELACHAUME (*moving above the sofa*) Nothing will stop me telling you, young woman, that Georges is ruining his life, because of you.
BARBARA (*suddenly coming forward*) You make me sick, all of you!

(*They all turn to face Barbara.* ISABELLE *moves to* R *of the sofa*)

JACQUES. Have some tact, for God's sake! Tact, Barbara, please!
BARBARA. You're nauseating, all three of you, with your terror of losing him. You know you'll soon get your hold on him again

and take him back home—isn't that enough for you? (*She pauses*) Answer me—isn't that enough?

JACQUES. My God! That takes the biscuit. Barbara defending Georges' love-affair with the beautiful stranger. Didn't I tell you it was pure novelette?

BARBARA. Why say anything at all to her? Why must you do any more breaking up and destroying? The poor girl's seen us, now. Aren't you satisfied? (*She moves below the piano*)

MME DELACHAUME. Barbara!

DELACHAUME (*not sure of what he has heard*) What did she say?

MME DELACHAUME (*moving* C) Barbara, my dear. You can't know what you're saying. Your jealousy's got the better of you.

BARBARA. I just want him left alone for a bit. I want him left alone, happy.

MME DELACHAUME. But, you're mad, my dear—you mean, *without us?*

BARBARA (*quietly*) Yes, without us.

MME DELACHAUME (*bursting out*) And that's what you call being in love with Georges? (*She moves to the window*)

(*There is a silence during which* ISABELLE *looks at* BARBARA)

ISABELLE (*softly*) But—who are you?

JACQUES (*bowing and clowning*) My wife. I don't know what I can have been thinking of when she came in. Do forgive me. (*He crosses to Barbara and takes her arm*) Allow me to introduce Mme Jeanette Lebos, known as Barbara, because she thinks it's posher. Say how-d'ye-do to the lady, now, Barbara. Pay your respects.

ISABELLE. Your wife? But . . .

JACQUES (*crossing towards Isabelle*) Oh, yes, there's a big *but*. When you scratch a bit below the surface there's always a *but* in life. (*He returns to Barbara*) Let me give you a tip. Never scratch —it's dangerous. Never, never scratch. Appearances are quite sufficient, they make a whole world in themselves.

(GEORGES *enters from the hall.* ISABELLE *runs to him.* DELACHAUME *moves below the sofa.* MME DELACHAUME *moves to* L *of the sofa*)

(*He sees Georges and shouts without the slightest confusion*) Isn't that right, old chap?

ISABELLE. Georges!

MME DELACHAUME (*almost at the same moment*) Georges, my boy. We've been looking everywhere for you.

DELACHAUME. You've got to be back before midnight. Do you hear? Absolutely got to.

GEORGES (*with a gesture*) Don't shout, Father, I've just come away from there. It's all settled. (*To Isabelle*) I see you've introduced yourselves.

ISABELLE. Yes, Georges.

SCENE 2   DINNER WITH THE FAMILY   47

GEORGES. This is Jacques, the famous Jacques. There is Jacques' wife. I'd never even mentioned her to you, it was very careless of me. My real father, my real mother. Where have the others gone?

ISABELLE. They're just outside. There are no more trains, so they can't leave until tomorrow morning.

GEORGES. Isn't that grand? Well, have you made your choice? Which parents would you like to pass the evening with? The false ones were quite charming, if only they'd known their parts. But the real ones aren't too bad, either, you'll see.

ISABELLE. Georges, why did you lie to me?

GEORGES. Haven't they told you I'm a married man?

ISABELLE. No, Georges.

GEORGES. Astonishing.

DELACHAUME. I hope that shows you that your parents have all the delicacy you seem to lack yourself, my boy. We've not said a thing.

GEORGES (*gently*) I am married, Isabelle.

ISABELLE (*tonelessly*) Are you, Georges?

GEORGES. I've been married four years, to a woman I don't love. A very rich woman. (*He smiles feebly. Still looking at Isabelle he orders his father*) You explain, Father. You're so good at explaining.

DELACHAUME (*not sure whether he is being laughed at or praised*) I'm good at explaining? Well, er—of course, I'm very proud of your marriage. Who wouldn't be? Have you ever heard of Desmond's Steel Girders, young lady?

ISABELLE (*still looking at Georges; stammering*) I—I—I couldn't say.

GEORGES (*quietly*) That's what I married—a Desmond Steel Girder.

DELACHAUME (*moving above the sofa*) The biggest firm of steel girders in Europe.

ISABELLE. Is that all, Georges?

GEORGES. No, Isabelle. We're all living on that marriage, Jacques and Barbara included. The reason they've followed me out here is that my wife has threatened to throw us all out on the street if I don't get home before midnight tonight.

MME DELACHAUME. Don't listen to him, he doesn't know what he's saying.

GEORGES. There's much worse to come. With us, you know, there's always worse to come . . .

ISABELLE (*stopping him with a gesture*) No, I don't want to hear, even from you.

(GEORGES *looks at Isabelle, his smile getting harder*)

GEORGES (*with a change of tone*) Afraid? (*He draws away backwards*) I've never known you afraid before.

Isabelle. I've never heard you laugh like that before. It's a nasty laugh. You're hurt.

(Georges *is silent*)

(*She moves to him*) Georges, have you the courage to stay alone with me just for five minutes?
  Georges. I've courage enough for anything tonight.
  Mme Delachaume (*coming forward*) Georges, my boy, I know this is a very difficult situation for you, very painful, in fact; but it's nearly eleven o'clock. Paris is twenty-five miles away and we might be held up on the road.
  Isabelle. Just five minutes, Georges. I think you owe me that.
  Georges (*to the others*) Leave us alone, please.

(*The others hesitate.*
  Barbara *exits to the hall.* Jacques *moves to* l *of the hall doors*)

(*He pushes Mme Delachaume and then Delachaume to the hall doors*) There's no need for any anxiety; in five minutes we'll all go back home together. Nothing can stop us doing that, now.
  Delachaume. All right. We'll trust you once again, for the last time. Do you hear? The last time. See you in five minutes, my boy.
  Georges. In five minutes, Father.

(Jacques, Delachaume *and* Mme Delachaume *exit to the hall.* Jacques, *as he goes, switches off the wall-brackets and closes the doors with a cynical servility on his face*)

(*He crosses to the sofa and sits*) What a let-down, isn't it? A young man of such good family, with so many qualities. Too many qualities, really, Isabelle. I wonder that didn't put you on your guard.
  Isabelle. Georges, why did you lie to me?
  Georges. It should be as clear as daylight. I meet a girl in the Louvre; for two months I go with her every day and visit the sights and monuments of Paris. It's one long idyll. You actually made me go round visiting old Paris and drinking tea. I hate tea, always did. Well, one day, I'd had too much of your tea and your little pink-and-gold tea-rooms. I was fed up with snatching kisses in a taxi and holding hands over a doughnut. But what could I do? What proposition could I possibly make to a serious little girl from the Pyrenees, lost in the capital of France, supposed to be studying literature? Show her the curiosities of Parisian life? No. Make love in a shady hotel? No. What could I offer you? They've told you, I'm a married man; there was nothing on earth I could decently offer. So, as I'm a pretty low species of human, really, I invented this nice young man, with a wonderful home, and an old and faithful servant, respectable parents—and I decided to seduce you, that's all.

Scene 2   DINNER WITH THE FAMILY   49

Isabelle (*gently*)   Did you really think I'd believe anything as silly as that?

Georges (*lowering his head*)   No, Isabelle, but—you can't blame me for trying.

Isabelle (*with one step towards him*)   Georges, why did you lie to me?

Georges.   Mm? (*He looks at her in silence for a moment. In a different tone*) Well, the first day I lied for the sad and sordid reason I've just given you. I liked you, you were a young girl. I wasn't going to tell you who I was, point-blank, and spoil it all.

Isabelle.   And the days that followed?

Georges.   Afterwards, I began lying so that it shouldn't look as though I'd lied too much on the first day. Then the nice young man you seemed to like so much would be real, to some extent.

Isabelle.   But why all this play-acting and fuss tonight, since I was going home tomorrow, anyway?

Georges (*smiling*)   Ah, tonight is altogether different. It's the little slip that always catches out the murderer and gets him hanged. He's got cast-iron alibis, he removes all traces of himself with every possible care, but he gives a kiddie a fifty franc piece as he leaves the house, or he picks a flower from the dead man's garden to wear in his buttonhole. (*He lowers his head like a boy caught red-handed in mischief*) Tonight's little manœuvre was pure selfishness, just for my own pleasure, Isabelle.

Isabelle (*with another step towards him*)   What pleasure?

Georges.   Oh, very simple, just passing a real family evening at home with you—and my people.

Isabelle (*moving to* L *of the sofa; half-surprised, half-amused*)   Do you think it's as enjoyable as all that, a simple family evening?

Georges.   I wouldn't know.

Isabelle.   You wouldn't know?

Georges (*gently*)   I try to imagine it sometimes. (*He is huddled on the sofa, hands in the pockets of his raincoat, his collar turned up and his eyes closed*)

(Isabelle *watches him for a moment, quite disarmed, then goes on questioning him*)

Isabelle.   You weren't brought up at home, then?

Georges.   Oh, yes.

Isabelle.   Didn't your parents get on very well together?

Georges.   Not very well, no. Mother was always out late having tea with her friends—she had so many friends. We were always waiting dinner for her. When it got late, I'd fall asleep at table and the maid used to hold me and give me my dinner. She was generally wild at having to feed me. Father was wild about it, too. So he'd go upstairs and lock himself in his room with his tin soldiers.

Isabelle.   *His* tin soldiers?

GEORGES. Yes. At my home it was father who always played with the soldiers. Oh, it was an odd house, I can tell you. Your mother and father were serious-minded people, I suppose?
ISABELLE. Yes, Georges.
GEORGES. And they all had their meals at the same time?
ISABELLE. Of course.
GEORGES (*not ironically*) That must have been marvellous. (*He looks at Isabelle for a moment, and smiles*) Actually, people have only to look at you to see that you were brought up in a house that was bright and warm in the evenings, and where the meals were calm and there was no quarrelling. My lovely, radiant Isabelle —what a lot of happy grandmothers you must have way back behind you, there, in one long line, holding on to each other's skirts—protecting you. (*He pauses and smiles gently*) It may sound funny, but I think I was a little bit in love with those grandmothers of yours, as well.

(ISABELLE *moves to Georges and kneels at his feet*)

ISABELLE (*softly*) In spite of all these other lies, then, Georges, it was true that you were in love with me?
GEORGES. Yes, Isabelle, *that* was true. (*He kisses her*)
ISABELLE (*sitting on the floor and leaning on Georges' knee*) Then I'm happy, and I don't care about the rest.
GEORGES. You're right. Let's be happy. (*He ponders a moment*) We always ask too much of life, you know. We begin by wanting a whole lifetime of happiness, then we learn that to have a few stolen years even is wonderful luck. Later, we reconcile ourselves to reality and could be satisfied with a single evening. Then suddenly we've only five minutes left, and we discover that even that is a boundless oasis in the desert, five minutes' happiness. (*He looks around them at the room, dark and yet friendly*) It's nice in my old home, isn't it? Mother and father have folded their newspapers at last and gone up to their rooms: and good old Jacques understood in the end, went off and left us alone. It's snug here. We've no need to hold hands, like beginners, to make sure the other one's still there in the darkness and silence. We're certain of each other being there. A peaceful end to a happy day. What shall we do tomorrow, darling?
ISABELLE. Lots of things, Georges.
GEORGES. Let's make it something silly. One of those unbelievable things that innocent lovers still do, the sort who don't know where to go in Paris. Visit the Invalides or the Eiffel Tower, or go boating in the Bois de Boulogne.
ISABELLE (*smiling*) We've been an ardent boating couple, haven't we, Georges?
GEORGES (*smiling*) Very ardent—but it was all according to plan. (*He raises his finger and sententiously plays the clown*) All engaged couples should take a course in the skiffs on the lake in the Bois

SCENE 2 DINNER WITH THE FAMILY 51

de Boulogne. They should learn in good time how to steer the ship of married life. You know, I'm going to be a drivelling old bore after we've been married about twenty years. Will you hate me?

ISABELLE. No.

GEORGES. No—I can see you. You'll be very sweet, very elegant and very charming. The faithful old companion. The woman who never even thought of dyeing her hair, and ignored every one of her wrinkles. Do you agree to keep all your wrinkles and let your hair grow white through love of me, Isabelle?

ISABELLE. Of course, Georges.

GEORGES (*sighing; relieved*) Ah, good! I felt I couldn't have lived through my five minutes' happiness without that guarantee. I would almost certainly have wasted them in making a scene. Maybe I'd better make a scene, anyway, on purpose, so that these five minutes really seem like a lifetime of happiness. What do you think?

ISABELLE (*smiling*) I think the wish is quite enough, darling.

GEORGES (*looking at her*) "Darling!" What wonderful courage. You've never called me that before, Isabelle.

ISABELLE (*bending her head and smiling*) I never dared to before. But we've been living together four whole minutes, already, so I—er . . .

GEORGES. Four minutes gone. How time flies! I was wondering where this confidence, this comfort, this feeling of peace had crept in. Of course, we've reached the stage of calm and tender affection —our golden wedding already. We've been very happy together, Isabelle, and, although we haven't said it very often, I think we've loved each other quite a lot.

ISABELLE (*in a slightly trembling voice*) Why are you putting it in the past tense?

GEORGES (*drawing back and smiling a trifle sadly*) Because our long married life is drawing to a close, Isabelle.

ISABELLE. Georges, darling—please don't pretend any more. I'm frightened now, Georges.

(JACQUES *enters from the hall*)

JACQUES. Excuse me, won't you? I must seem like the jailer in a melodrama. (*He crosses to* L *of the sofa*) The five minutes are up, Georges, your father and mother are out in the car already.

(GEORGES *and* ISABELLE *rise.*
BARBARA *enters slowly from the hall*)

ISABELLE. Georges, please. (*She throws herself distracted into his arms*)

(GEORGES *looks at Isabelle, smiles, strokes her and pats her like a frightened child.* BARBARA *moves below the piano*)

GEORGES. Don't be frightened, Isabelle. Leave me alone with them for a moment. I'll settle everything, I promise you. (*He leads her to the hall doors, holding her shoulder*)

(ISABELLE *exits to the hall*)

(*He brusquely closes the doors and moves to Barbara*) Stay behind after we've left, will you? Tell her I lied to her again, because I was afraid of seeing her hurt. Tell her I don't love her and have never loved her, that she'd better go back home and forget all about this wretched little interlude as soon as she can.

(JACQUES *moves to Georges, slaps him and grips him on the shoulder*)

JACQUES. Aren't you the lucky one not to be sentimental. Lucky fellow!

GEORGES (*quietly*) Jacques, take your hand off my shoulder, damn you! (*He falls forward on to the piano*)

BARBARA (*leaning over Georges*) What's the matter?

GEORGES. Unbutton the coat, will you, please?

(BARBARA *opens Georges' raincoat*)

BARBARA (*with a cry*) Georges, you're covered with blood.

GEORGES (*with his eyes closed; tonelessly*) Don't touch it. My shirt's stuck to me. Just unbutton the coat.

(BARBARA *opens Georges' coat*)

BARBARA. It's a bullet wound, Georges?

GEORGES. It's not serious. It was Christine. You know her little pearl-handled revolver? Well, this time she used it. We had a terrible scene. I tried to take it off her and in the struggle, she fell back against the marble fireplace. Everybody started to scream and shout; I rushed back here. I may have killed her.

JACQUES. My God! We must go back at once. Can you walk?

GEORGES. I think I need a stiff drink.

JACQUES. A drink? Where the devil do you think I can find a drink in this place?

GEORGES. Call the butler.

(JACQUES *moves up* C *and rings the bell.*
The BUTLER *enters by the secret door down* R. BARBARA *helps* GEORGES *to the chair* LC *and kneels* R *of him*)

BUTLER. Did you ring, sir?

JACQUES (*crossing to the butler*) Have you got anything really strong to drink here? Perhaps a liqueur?

BUTLER (*with a smile*) Oh, sir. What a question! (*He strikes an attitude and recites*)

"To every meal the epicure
   Takes choicest wine and best liqueur;

SCENE 2   DINNER WITH THE FAMILY

> The House of Dufort, when you dine,
> Will see to all liqueurs and wine."

We have every possible liqueur, sir, and in particular a special old Calvados we highly recommend.

GEORGES. No, I'd like some rum.

BUTLER (*caught*) Ah! Of course, just the thing we haven't got. Nobody ever drinks it nowadays.

(GEORGES *rises unsteadily and helped by* BARBARA *moves slowly towards the hall doors.* JACQUES *moves to the hall doors and opens them*)

Oh, just a moment—we have a thing called Rum Fantasy in the kitchen, which I was going to use for lighting the omelette, had everything passed off in the normal way. But I'd never recommend it, sir, for ordinary consumption.

GEORGES. We'll go down. Bring your bottle of Rum Fantasy out to the car, will you?

BUTLER (*crossing to the hall doors*) How many glasses, sir? One, two, three?

(JACQUES, GEORGES *and* BARBARA *exit to the hall, without answering the Butler*)

(*He turns and moves* C. *Stunned*) Rum Fantasy—and probably drunk out of the bottle. (*He shudders with disgust and moves to the secret door down* R. *With arms raised to Heaven*) What an evening! What an evening!

The BUTLER *exits down* R *as—*

the CURTAIN *falls*

ACT III

SCENE—*The drawing-room at Senlis. An hour or so later.*

When the CURTAIN *rises,* BARBARA *and* ISABELLE *are standing motionless in front of the hall doors, which are wide open. They appear to be waiting for something. After a few moments, the* PROPRIETRESS *enters the hall from* L. *She carries a bowl and some cotton-wool.*

PROPRIETRESS. We'll soon be finished. The doctor says it's quite a superficial wound.

(*The* PROPRIETRESS *exits up the stairs*)

BARBARA (*moving to the table* L *of the doors and facing up stage*) Do you think it's very painful?

ISABELLE. Not very, I shouldn't think.

BARBARA. I wouldn't like it to hurt him *very much*. He's been awfully spoilt.

(ISABELLE *wanders to the left end of the sofa. There is a pause*)

(*She turns and faces Isabelle. Suddenly*) You *are* in love with him, aren't you?

ISABELLE. Why do you ask?

BARBARA. You seem so calm. (*She moves* C) He's in love with you, you know. He was lying to me just now. It's you he's been looking for.

ISABELLE (*shrugging her shoulders*) What do you know about it?

BARBARA (*with a sad smile; gently*) I know him very well.

ISABELLE (*after a pause*) You were his mistress, weren't you?

BARBARA (*moving to the piano*) I wouldn't ask any more questions, if I were you. (*She takes a cigarette from the case on the piano and lights it*) You know he loves you—so does it matter now what he used to be to any of us? (*She sits in the chair* LC)

ISABELLE. You're quite right, it's of no importance to me.

BARBARA. He was everything you'd hate—everything that he'll never be again if only he goes away with you tomorrow and leaves all this behind.

ISABELLE (*moving to the hall doors*) So you're not quite sure whether he'll go with me or not?

BARBARA. Not yet, no. There's still a faint chance for me. It's a mean little chance, I'm afraid, very mean, and I don't intend to tell you what it is.

ISABELLE. Do you think you can frighten me with your mean little chance?

BARBARA. Oh, I haven't the slightest desire to . . .

ISABELLE. You're going to try and keep him for yourself, I

know that. Seize on him as soon as you can—that's what you're waiting for. (*She moves and sits on the left arm of the sofa*)
BARBARA. No—I shan't try.
ISABELLE. It would surprise me if you let him go, just like that.
BARBARA. The others will try, probably, but I shan't. I've nothing more I want to say to him.
ISABELLE. I suppose you get a kick out of behaving as if you're making me a present of him?
BARBARA. Oh, no. I'm not the "saintly" type. Besides, I couldn't give you my Georges, the one I know; you would never want him.
ISABELLE. You think not?
BARBARA. I'm sure of it. He's not at all a nice young man, my Georges, he's everything you'd hate. He's sad, he's never sure of anything. He's unfair. He's cruel.
ISABELLE. You're lying.
BARBARA. Yes. *He* lies, too. *He's* a liar. (*She rises, moves to the piano and studies the photograph on it*) He makes appointments and forgets to turn up. He never keeps his promises. He's petty and mean and complains and quarrels all the time. He's a strange man, *my* Georges.
ISABELLE. What good can it do you to run him down like this?
BARBARA (*smiling*) That's not running him down—that's the way I loved him.

(*There is a silence during which they look at each other*)

ISABELLE (*suddenly*) You must hate me. Don't you?
BARBARA. No. It's funny, I hated you with all my heart at first, when he was always searching for you and hadn't found you —but I must have used up all my hate; now that he's found you, for good, I realize that I don't hate you any more.
ISABELLE. I hate *you*.

(*The* DOCTOR *enters in the hall from* L. *He carries a small bag*)

BARBARA (*moving to the Doctor*) Have you finished, Doctor?
DOCTOR. Yes, madame. It's only a scratch, really. See that he rests and is quiet, so that his temperature doesn't go up.

(BARBARA *turns away*)

(*He bows. To them both*) Would you be good enough to show me the way out?

(*They hesitate, then* ISABELLE *suddenly decides*)

ISABELLE (*rising*) I'll show you, Doctor.

(ISABELLE *and the* DOCTOR *go into the hall and exit to* R. BARBARA *moves to the hall doors, pauses, then crosses to the windows and stands looking out.*
GEORGES *enters in the hall from* L)

GEORGES (*anxiously*) Where is she?

BARBARA (*smiling a little*) She's still here. She'll be back in a moment. Lie down, Georges. The doctor said you must rest.

GEORGES (*moving to the sofa and sitting on it*) What a stupid thing to happen. If only I'd fainted a bit later, in the car, you wouldn't have brought me back *here*.

BARBARA (*moving behind the sofa*) Are you feeling better? The doctor didn't hurt you very much?

GEORGES. No. Where has she gone?

BARBARA. To show the doctor out. (*She pauses. Suddenly*) What are you going to do, Georges?

GEORGES. I don't know. (*Softly*) It isn't up to me to decide what I'm going to do. (*He pauses*) How long is it since Jacques left?

BARBARA. Nearly an hour.

GEORGES. He should have phoned by now.

BARBARA. But there's no phone here. I had to ring through before to the house next door. Jacques probably hasn't thought of doing that.

> (BARBARA *looks at Georges in silence. Suddenly her thoughts bring tears to her eyes.* GEORGES *sees* BARBARA, *who turns her head away, so does he*)

GEORGES (*stretching out on the sofa*) I wish you wouldn't cry, Barbara.

BARBARA. I'm not crying.

GEORGES. Oh, don't pretend. What were you thinking about?

BARBARA (*not daring to look at him*) Just the way you and I used to play cops and robbers, when we first went out together. (*She moves up* C) Do you remember? We said we were being followed. We were on the run. (*She moves above the sofa*) We kept jumping in and out of taxis, and before we ever went into a café —took the most elaborate precautions. Now you play cops and robbers with someone else.

(GEORGES *does not reply*)

(*She hangs her head and continues, gently and ashamed*) I hope with all my heart that you won't have to go to prison, Georges. (*She moves to the window and gazes out*) And I'm being very fair when I hope that. I can't help thinking that if you did go to prison, I'd be the one waiting at the gates when you came out. (*She turns to him*) You're disgusted with me, I expect?

(GEORGES *does not reply*)

(*After a pause*) You don't even want to answer me?

(GEORGES *closes his eyes.*)
    ISABELLE *enters from the hall, moves to the sofa and looks down at Georges*)

ISABELLE (*to Barbara*) He's dropped off to sleep exhausted by the loss of blood, I suppose.
BARBARA (*with a little mysterious smile*) No, I don't think so, he always goes to sleep when he's unhappy.
ISABELLE. Why?
BARBARA. To stop being unhappy. It's a little trick he has.
ISABELLE. A trick?
BARBARA. Yes. He has several little tricks like that. Hasn't he ever begun drinking madly, with you, at about four o'clock in the afternoon?
ISABELLE. No, never.
BARBARA (*crossing to the piano*) Hasn't he ever laughed too loudly all of a sudden for no reason? Started to roar out his barrack-room songs enough to split your ear-drums? When he has to be gay, whatever the cost, much too gay?
ISABELLE. No.
BARBARA. You see. We're not talking about the same man at all.

(JACQUES *enters the hall from* R *and comes quickly into the room*)

(*She rushes to Jacques*) Well, what's the news?

(ISABELLE *moves towards Jacques*)

JACQUES. Where is he?
BARBARA (*indicating the sofa*) There, asleep.
JACQUES. Well, now, isn't that wonderful! We rush around the streets in the dead of night worried out of our wits; we sweat ourselves dizzy with plans for escape, alibis and what have you, and meantime M. Georges feels a bit tired, so he drops off to sleep.
BARBARA. Oh, come on, tell us what's happened.
JACQUES (*not paying any attention to her*) Do you know, I wish *he* was asking me that, pleading with me—I'd take my time and play the breathless messenger in a tragedy, who runs on and dithers. You know. (*He falls to his knees and waves his arms in dramatic gestures*) "It's awful—dreadful—I can't bring myself to say it—awful."
BARBARA (*hitting Jacques*) Tell us, for goodness sake.
JACQUES (*rising; with a change of tone*) Well—can you credit it? It was the merest bump. Only left a baby bruise. And the little wifie more in love than ever.

(BARBARA *turns away.* ISABELLE *stands up* L *of the sofa*)

(*He crosses to the piano and sits on the keyboard*) Now, poor soul, she thinks that he must absolutely adore her to go so far as to risk a criminal offence. Dear Edgar suggested that one to her—I must say the old boy doesn't lack imagination.
BARBARA. Where are those two?

JACQUES. I left them sitting on the end of Christine's bed, engaged—rather prematurely, I think—in killing the fatted calf.
ISABELLE. Rather prematurely, as you say. Georges has decided to go with me to the Pyrenees.
JACQUES. You're taking him away?
ISABELLE. Yes.
JACQUES. What for? To start bee-keeping?
ISABELLE. No, to start being my lover—and my husband as soon as the divorce is settled.
JACQUES (*rising, crossing and looking down at Georges*) What a delicate little bloom he is. The gentleman feels in need of a rest-cure in the country; so with a graceful shrug he drops us and takes the next train out of town.

(JACQUES *crosses to* BARBARA *and they move up* R *of the piano*)

(*Clowning*) Can we put forward any objection, do you think, to the gentleman going away for a rest-cure, my dear?
BARBARA (*half jokingly, half dreamily*) I don't think so.
JACQUES. What, then, remains for us to do, my dear?
BARBARA. Go away.
JACQUES. With dignity?
BARBARA. With dignity.
JACQUES. A gallant French exit—a smile, a hand on your heart, a foot at your behind. (*He moves to the hall doors and takes out his handkerchief*) Handkerchief held high for the last farewell: "Goodbye! And pray be happy, for you have deserved to be. You will never hear of us again." (*He stops short and moves to Isabelle*) No, for God's sake! Did you really think it would be as easy as that? Just scoot off to bliss with your gay Lothario by the first convenient train? Ha! I must laugh. Ha, ha, ha, ha! Do you hear me? I'm laughing. (*He lies on the floor below the chair* LC) And I'm making myself comfortable.
ISABELLE (*moving to Jacques*) What are you doing?
JACQUES. Waiting for him. Listen. Take my advice. I quite like you. Do you know what I'd do if I were in your place? Skidaddle. Before he wakes up.
ISABELLE (*coldly*) Really? And why?
JACQUES (*rising*) He's in love with you, of course, we know that. It's all hot, and sparkling, all bubble and squeak for joy at the moment. But he's not totally mad. Georges always comes back in the end, when he has to. And I see no earthly reason why he shouldn't come back this time.
ISABELLE. I think this time you'll add to your experience. Georges won't come back.
JACQUES. If you were a sensible girl, you'd believe me. I know him. He's done this trick at least a dozen times before.
ISABELLE (*moving below the sofa*) Be quiet, I won't listen to you.

Act III DINNER WITH THE FAMILY

JACQUES (*crossing and standing behind Isabelle*) You're making a mistake, I'm trying to save you making an ass of yourself, my dear. This sleeping beauty here is a wolf in sheep's clothing, a Casanova. I imagine yours is one of those straightforward lives, everything simple and clear. Go to the station alone, tomorrow. Jump in the train and go back to your bees, your big dogs and your virtuous grannies down on the farm. (*He kneels c and implores her*) For the sake of your virtuous grannies, sweet lady.

ISABELLE (*moving R, shrugging*) You're just being a bore.

JACQUES (*rising and moving up L of the sofa*) I'm boring myself, too. I'm wearing myself out taking all this trouble with you— but only because I feel it is my duty. In your eyes, I'm a despicable sort of cad, I know, but doesn't it mean anything to you, that a cad like me with God knows what presentiment of evil— goes to such lengths trying to warn you?

ISABELLE (*moving above the sofa and looking down at Georges*) No. It doesn't mean a thing.

JACQUES. You're a hard woman. If I were in your place I'd find it overwhelming. Honestly, do you believe he loves you enough to cast his old wolf-skin, chuck it out of the window and turn overnight into an absolute lamb?

ISABELLE. Yes, I do believe it, with all my heart. I believe I can teach him real happiness.

JACQUES. As if happiness were a thing anyone can learn. You'll need an inhuman amount of talent. (*He crosses to Barbara*) Still, how touching it all is. Don't you think so? (*To Barbara*) Aren't you moved? I am, I really am.

ISABELLE. You're only saying that because you hate him.

JACQUES (*suddenly tired of it all*) No, I'm not even sure I hate him any longer. I've said it too often without doing anything about it. It's just so much hot air. A few moments ago, when I started talking, I knew I wouldn't convince you, I knew he'd go away with you, but I kept on so that he'd wake up and throw me out. You see—once I start talking and get really wound up, there's always got to be somebody to stop me by force and throw me out. And, mind you, they're doing me a favour. Otherwise, I go on and on and wade in deeper and deeper till I wear myself out and feel as bad as my victims about it all.

BARBARA (*after a pause*) Come on. It's not worth the trouble waiting till he wakes up.

JACQUES. Think not? (*Very business-like*) In that case, I will be brief. (*He crosses to Isabelle*) The end of this month is going to be extremely difficult for us. Do you think you could lend me fifty thousand francs?

ISABELLE. You must think I'm rich, too—I haven't got any money, you know.

JACQUES (*modestly*) Five thousand?

ISABELLE (*nearly laughing*) Five thousand, perhaps—(*she moves to the window seat, picks up her bag and returns to Jacques*)—I've got just about that much in my handbag. (*She takes a note from her handbag*)

BARBARA (*crossing to Isabelle and snatching the bag and money*) Jacques!

JACQUES. What the hell's up with you? Are you mad?

BARBARA (*replacing the note in the bag*) Not in the least. (*She crosses to the piano*)

JACQUES (*following Barbara*) Oh, what a delightful gesture, my dear. It'll make a wonderful story. I shall tell everyone, depend upon it, especially the waiters in the cheap restaurants we shall be reduced to from next week onwards. I can see them being so impressed they'll shower us with steak and chips. But you've made your gesture now—so keep out of this, will you? (*He pushes her aside*) Do forgive her, it was just a thoughtless impulse.

BARBARA. No, Jacques.

JACQUES. She was only helping us through a difficult patch.

BARBARA. Well, I don't want her help.

JACQUES (*sitting in the chair LC; completely discouraged*) If we all played at being noble, we'd never get anywhere at all. There must be some noble people in the world, of course, but not too many, don't overcrowd 'em.

BARBARA (*after a pause; suddenly*) You're quite right, Jacques, I'm a fool. If we all play at being noble, we'll never get anywhere. Georges especially—he'll never get anywhere at all. (*She crosses to Jacques*) I'll take that money. It will make it easier for him that way. (*She takes the note from the bag, hands it to Jacques, then returns the bag to Isabelle*)

JACQUES. Hurrah! Let's leave it at that.

(GEORGES *moves*)

Careful, he's waking. (*He quickly pockets the note*)

GEORGES (*sitting up and looking around*) Where are mother and father?

JACQUES (*rising and moving to L of the sofa*) With Christine. And she's as fit as a fiddle. Only a bump, old chap, you can start all over again tomorrow.

(GEORGES *gives a deep sigh. You feel he is suddenly filled with a hard kind of joy*)

GEORGES. I never want to go back there again. I don't want anything I've got there. Tomorrow I'm going to put on a different suit, and tie and shoes and shirt, get on the train, and go right away from here.

JACQUES. We know.

GEORGES (*savagely*) Why did you come back, then?

JACQUES. To wish you God speed, dear boy. (*He sits on the left arm of the sofa*) Whether we adore each other or not is beside the point. We've still got to come to some arrangement.

GEORGES (*shrugging*) You can tell mother and father that I shall be back in Paris soon to settle the details of the divorce. Tell them I'm going to find a job and start work, then I shall help them as much as I can. (*He pauses*) Perhaps father had better look round for something to do.

JACQUES. He'll look round all right, never you fear. He's been looking round for the last thirty years. But it's so hard to find a well-paid easy job, nowadays.

GEORGES. I'll give them all I have left. They'll go to an hotel at first, I expect. Mother will want to put up in a palace, of course, as usual, so as not to sink too far in her friends' esteem. And father will gaily agree, thinking the price they quote for the room is by the week, not by the day, and that drinks, coffee, cigars and everything else is included.

JACQUES. The old boy is two or three wars behind us.

GEORGES. Try to make them see that they're old, now, and should be sensible; they must manage to live for at least a few months on what I send. (*He rises and moves to Isabelle. With a smile*) You'll forgive all these details, I know.

ISABELLE. You should forgive me for staying and listening. I'd better leave you for a bit, Georges. (*She moves to the hall doors*)

GEORGES (*following her to the doors*) Thanks, Isabelle. We shan't be long.

(ISABELLE *exits to the hall.* GEORGES *closes the doors. They all look at one another, embarrassed*)

(*He moves to* L *of Jacques*) So there we are.

JACQUES (*rising; echoing him*) There we are, as you say.

GEORGES. What are you two going to do?

JACQUES. In the words of the old artist, Edgar himself—we shall "take steps", old chap.

GEORGES. Will Barbara have to go to work?

BARBARA. None of your business.

GEORGES. I'll go into what money there still is and see that you have something.

JACQUES. Thanks. Actually, it's embarrassing having to tell you this at a time when we're all so upset, but I was going to mention it to you tonight at dinner. I've had the tailor's bill—you know, for the—er . . .

GEORGES. Right, I'll send you that.

JACQUES (*softly*) Fifteen thousand francs.

GEORGES. But you told me it was going to be thirty thousand?

JACQUES (*hanging his head*) Yes, but it's fifteen thousand.

GEORGES (*smiling*) Good God, Jacques! Don't tell me you're turning honest, too?

JACQUES (*moving down* R *of the sofa*) Everybody's honest in one way or another. The trouble is, there's only one official way.

(*There is a pause. They are uncomfortable*)
So there we are.

GEORGES (*sitting in the chair* LC *and looking at Barbara*) As you say, there we are.

(*There is a silence*)

JACQUES (*crossing to Georges; suddenly breaking the silence*) There's one thing I'd like to know. Why did you tell her I saved your life once in a boat, a long time ago?

GEORGES. Have you forgotten one day when we were in Brittany—there was a strong current and I thought I'd never get back in my depth? You were green with fright but you managed to get the canoe out to me for all that. (*He pauses*) We were only twelve, then.

JACQUES. How time flies.

(*There is a silence*)

(*Suddenly and in a different tone*) Look here, it's all finished, now— (*he moves down* R) so we're not going to quarrel over a detail. (*He moves above the sofa towards the hall doors*) If I'm in the way for your good-byes to Barbara, I can disappear.

BARBARA (*throwing herself into Jacques' arms; with a cry*) No, don't leave us. (*Still clinging to Jacques, she turns to Georges*) She'll be getting anxious, Georges, I'm sure you ought to call her back.

GEORGES (*rising and moving to Barbara*) Yes. But I wanted to say good-bye to you, Barbara.

BARBARA. You said it, five minutes ago.

GEORGES. But we can't just part like that.

BARBARA. Yes, we can. I tell you, we can. (*She almost shouts*) Why pretend we've anything in common any more? What have our troubles to do with you? You can't bear the sight of us, now. I've known that longer than you've known it yourself. Well, hurry up and throw us out. This hurts.

GEORGES (*gently*) It hurts me, too.

BARBARA (*after a moment; gently*) I hope it does, Georges.

GEORGES. It does. But all the same, I must say good-bye properly. I'm leaving you, Barbara—for ever.

BARBARA (*with a gulp*) For ever. Yes.

GEORGES. When a man gives a woman up, the usual thing is to promise to be friends, to soften the parting. I'm not promising you my friendship. (*He lowers his voice. It is difficult for him to say and he says it even with a touch of tenderness*) I can only promise you my feeling of shame—my hatred of what we were to each other, Barbara.

BARBARA (*quietly*) Your "hatred", yes.

GEORGES. The whole bunch of us around Christine led disgraceful lives; but we two were the worst. The others were only thinking of money, but we two—in the midst of the petty wrangling and all the dirty little bargains that went on—you and I went through the motions of love.

BARBARA (*more quietly still*) The motions; yes.

GEORGES (*moving to the piano; suddenly*) Forgive me, Barbara.

BARBARA (*after a slight pause; looking up*) What for?

GEORGES (*dully*) For the foul life I made you lead.

(BARBARA, *shaken by a shudder of tenderness, smiles, breaks from Jacques and moves to Georges*)

BARBARA. No, Georges—I can only *thank* you for that foul life, as you call it.

(*There is a terrible silence*)

(*She suddenly cries out and rushes to the hall doors*) I'll fetch her back to you.

GEORGES (*running to Barbara and catching her*) Barbara!

BARBARA (*turning on him*) What is it? What more do you want me to say—that—that horrible sordid life was simple for me, as simple as this girl's happiness is to her, just because I was in love with you? Do you think that will make it any easier afterwards? (*She frees herself, opens the hall doors and calls*) Isabelle.

(ISABELLE *enters from the hall*)

(*She takes Isabelle by the arm and stands her in front of Georges*) We're just leaving. We're in absolute agreement, my husband and I, on everything. Thank you for the money.

GEORGES (*leaping at this*) What money?

JACQUES (*trying to interpose*) Nothing! Nothing at all! A joke. Just a joke. A mistake.

BARBARA (*face to face with Georges*) It's something to make up for what we're losing from Christine. You don't think we'd just leave you without getting any money, do you? Really! What do you take us for?

GEORGES. I forbid you to take anything from her. I'll send you everything I've got.

JACQUES (*shrugging*) That's a good one—you've got nothing, now.

(BARBARA *bursts into false laughter which suddenly stops. She then asks feverishly as though something were on her mind and she were in a violent hurry*)

BARBARA. Well, Jacques?

JACQUES. Yes, dear?

BARBARA. Why can't we go? What the devil are we waiting for?

E*

JACQUES. True enough. Grace, my dear, style before all things. (*He bows like a cavalier*) Young lady . . .

(DELMONTE *and* MME DE MONTRACHET *appear at the hall doors. The* BUTLER *is behind them*)

Come in, ladies and gentlemen. (*He leads Isabelle down* R *of the sofa and returns to Mme de Montrachet*) Don't think twice about it. (*He leads Mme de Montrachet to the chair* LC, *moves the chair down* R *of the piano and turns it to face* R) Walk right in.

(MME DE MONTRACHET *sits in the chair*)

Don't be afraid, please, you're at home here, you know.

(DELMONTE *moves and stands above Mme de Montrachet.* BARBARA *moves down* C. *The* BUTLER *stands below the table up* C. GEORGES *crosses and stands above Isabelle*)

Come in, come in. This is the home of happiness, dignity and every pleasure in the calendar that has a proper licence. (*He takes Barbara by the hand, leads her down* R, *swings her round to face the others and stands behind her*) Look at that, isn't it lovely? There you have the Family with a capital F. The pure Family with nothing to be ashamed of. Doesn't it just belch fine sentiments—or, at any rate, it *pretends* pretty well. And that's the main thing for a family, after all.

DELMONTE. What do you want with us, sir? Really, I don't know what's taken hold of you. This is farcical!

JACQUES (*without a smile*) No, not farcical, sir—it's tragic. You're an actor, I take it, sir?

DELMONTE. I am.

JACQUES. Well, you've just come in time to give us some advice. (*He leads Barbara down* C)

(BARBARA *and* JACQUES *face upstage*)

Our scene has just come to an end, you see: now, how do you think we should make our exit?

DELMONTE. Well—hm—an exit isn't as easy as all that, you know. Not a simple thing at all, an exit. It depends on the situation, the character, and so on. What sort of parts have you been playing?

JACQUES. The villains.

DELMONTE. Ah, ah! There are some lovely exits you can use for villains. Albert Lambert used to go out draping himself in his cape . . .

(JACQUES *and* BARBARA *swing round to face downstage and move back slightly*)

JACQUES. I'm only wearing a jacket, it's not quite ample enough. (*He foolishly flaps his jacket*)

DELMONTE. Poor old Sylvain—he's dead—in *Arnolph*, used to exit running—(*he runs down* L) without a glance at anyone else on the stage.
JACQUES (*still withdrawing towards the doors*) That won't do. We want a view of every single face until the very last second.
MME DE MONTRACHET. Sarah Bernhardt never went out at all. She just stayed on the stage for the final curtain and the applause.
JACQUES (*still withdrawing*) There'll be no applause for us. Besides, we've just *got* to have an exit.
DELMONTE. Well—er—Mounet was wonderful. When he wanted a good exit—(*he moves down* C) he used to march to the footlights first . . .
JACQUES (*at the hall doors*) Too dangerous.

(DELMONTE *moves to the window*)

Well, don't bother thinking up any more. We've covered the four yards to the door. Those last four yards before disappearing, that sometimes takes years to cover. (*He pauses*) Well—nobody moved? We're going. (*He pauses*) Nobody spoke? One—two . . .
BARBARA (*looking at Georges; gently*) Nobody.
JACQUES. Well, then! Hey presto!

(JACQUES *and* BARBARA *exit to the hall, closing the doors behind them*)

DELMONTE (*crossing to the hall doors*) Dreadful! Impossible! No actor would ever make an exit like that. (*He goes to the window and gazes out*)
ISABELLE (*happily*) They've gone, Georges.
GEORGES. Yes, Isabelle.
ISABELLE. You're going to be free to live, now.
GEORGES (*sitting on the right arm of the sofa*) Yes, Isabelle, I shall be free to live, now.

(*The slam of a car door is heard off*)

(*He shudders*) What's that?
ISABELLE. Nothing. The car door slamming to.

(*They listen motionless for a moment*)

There! The engine's cold. It won't start. Ah! Now, it's started. It's moving away. It's at the end of the street already. It's passed the light from the last lamp-post. It's gone into the night, now. It doesn't exist any longer.

(GEORGES *looks at Isabelle*)

GEORGES (*with a frightened smile; murmuring*) You are terrifying, Isabelle.
ISABELLE. I am happiness. There's always something terrifying about happiness.

BUTLER (*coming forward*) Excuse me, sir, but would it be possible, do you think, now, for me to announce dinner?
ISABELLE. Yes, at once.

(DELMONTE *moves down* R)

BUTLER. At last! (*He makes the announcement as though nothing had happened*) Dinner is served.

(DELMONTE *crosses to* C. MME DE MONTRACHET *rises, meets him and takes his arm. They move to the hall doors*)

MME DE MONTRACHET. Ah! Come, children. It's five minutes to midnight. I think this is going to be a very odd sort of meal.

BUTLER. You are mistaken, madame, definitely mistaken. (*He recites*)

"A miracle, just one more
From the firm of Jean Dufort
Time and distance trouble not.
Nothing warmed up, all quite cold."

Oh, I'm sorry. I meant to say "hot", of course.

DELMONTE. Don't worry your head about that, old chap, please. No fuss. After all, it's only a little family dinner.

GEORGES *rises*.

DELMONT *and* MME DE MONTRACHET *exit to the hall*.
GEORGES *and* ISABELLE *follow them off*.
The BUTLER *goes last, closing the doors behind him as*—

the CURTAIN *falls*

FURNITURE AND PROPERTY LIST

ACT I

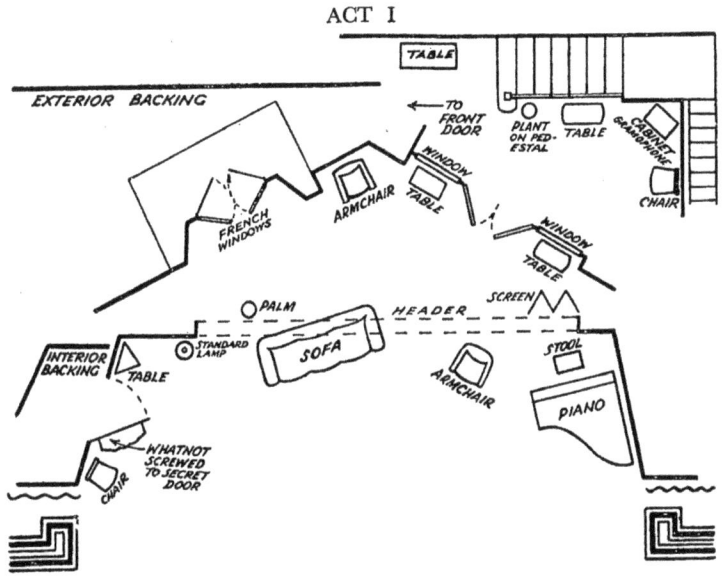

On stage—Small chair (down R)
    Whatnot (affixed to secret door) *In it:* ornaments
    Table (R) *On it:* portrait, ornament
    Standard lamp
    Tall palm on stand
    Sofa. *On it:* cushions
    Red damask window curtains
    Small armchair (up C)
    Table (up C) *On it:* table-lamp, telephone, ashtray, matches, maga-
            zine rack
    Table (up L) *On it:* vase, ornaments, musical box
    Folding screen
    Piano stool
    Baby Grand piano. *On it:* green shawl, ashtray, lighter
    Small armchair (LC)
    2 electric wall-brackets
    Carpet on floor
    Light switches at doors up LC
    In hall: pictures on walls
            table. *On it:* ornaments
            cabinet gramophone. *On it:* statuette
            small chair
            table. *On it:* ornaments
            potted fern on pedestal
            stair carpet
            hall carpet

68 DINNER WITH THE FAMILY

Secret door closed
Windows open and shutters open
Doors up LC open
Light fittings off

Off stage—Inventory (PROPRIETRESS)
　　　　　Small attaché case. *In it:* manuscript music, 2 books, photograph,
　　　　　　　small marble bust wrapped in muslin
　　　　　　　(GEORGES)
　　　　　Small attaché case. *In it:* beard, copy of "La Vie Parisienne" and
　　　　　　　"Figaro" (DELMONTE)
　　　　　Raincoat (GEORGES)
　　　　　Tray. *On it:* 2 glasses of sherry (BUTLER)

Personal—GEORGES: watch, fountain pen, 2 thousand franc notes, 1 five thou-
　　　　　sand franc note, case with cigarettes, lighter
　　　　　MME DE MONTRACHET: handbag. *In it:* knitting
　　　　　DELMONTE: Legion of Honour rosette

ACT II

SCENE 1

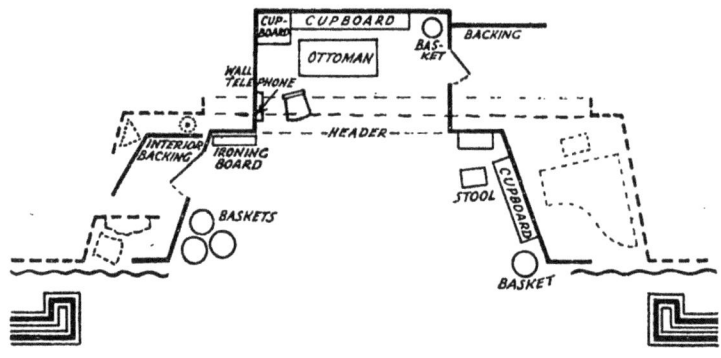

On stage—Ottoman
　　　　　Chair (up R)
　　　　　Stool (L)
　　　　　Wall telephone
　　　　　Laundry baskets

Off stage—Man's hat (MME DELACHAUME)
　　　　　Tray. *On it:* cloth, cup of camomile tea (DELACHAUME)

Personal—DELACHAUME: monocle, overcoat, top hat, cigar
　　　　　JACQUES: comb, case with cigarettes, lighter

SCENE 2

Setting as Act I

Strike—Book, sherry glasses

Set—*On chair up* C: Isabelle's hat
Secret door closed
Windows and shutters open
Doors up LC open
Light fittings on

Personal—ISABELLE: gloves, handbag. *In it:* 5 thousand franc notes
       BUTLER: bill, pencil

ACT III

Set—*On back of sofa:* Georges' raincoat
   On piano: cigarette-case with cigarettes, lighter
Secret door closed
Windows and shutters open
Doors up LC open
Light fittings on

Off stage—Bowl, cottonwool (PROPRIETRESS)
       Medical bag (DOCTOR)

Personal—JACQUES: handkerchief
      ISABELLE: handbag. *In it:* five thousand franc note

LIGHTING PLOT

Property Fittings Required—2 electric wall-brackets, table-lamp, standard lamp

ACT I Interior. A drawing-room and hall
  THE MAIN ACTING AREAS ARE—up LC, down LC, RC and at a sofa RC
  THE APPARENT SOURCES OF LIGHT ARE—in daytime, french windows up RC and at night, a table-lamp up C, a standard lamp RC and wall-brackets up RC and down L

To open: Effect of early evening sunshine
  Fittings off

Cue 1	GEORGES: ". . . lies to life."	(page 20)
	Slow fade of general lighting for sunset effect	
Cue 2	GEORGES: ". . . climbing trees."	(page 22)
	Continue fade of lights for twilight effect	
Cue 3	BUTLER closes shutters	(page 24)
	Reduce general lighting except for areas around hall door and to R of piano	

ACT II SCENE 1 Interior. An inset linen-room
  THE MAIN ACTING AREAS COVER THE WHOLE INSET
  THERE IS NO APPARENT SOURCE OF LIGHT

To open: All lights full up
No cues

ACT II SCENE 2 The drawing-room. Night
To open: Night effect outside windows
  Fittings on
  No light in hall

Cue 4	JACQUES switches off wall-brackets	(page 48)
	Snap out wall-brackets	
	Snap out on-stage lights except for lights covering the sofa and area between the sofa and doors	
Cue 5	ISABELLE: "Lots of things, Georges."	(page 50)
	Bring up lights slowly to cover area below piano	

ACT III The drawing-room. Night
To open: Night effect outside windows
  Fittings on

No cues

EFFECTS PLOT

ACT I

Cue 1	PROPRIETRESS: "... flowers *and birds.*" *Front door bell rings*	(page 5)
Cue 2	GEORGES: "... don't worry." *Front door bell rings*	(page 8)
Cue 3	GEORGES: "... lies to life." *Clock strikes 8*	(page 20)
Cue 4	DELMONTE: "... a larger fee." *Front door bell rings twice*	(page 21)
Cue 5	BUTLER: "No." *Front door bell rings*	(page 25)
Cue 6	MME DE MONTRACHET: "... ringing at the door." *Front door bell rings*	(page 25)

ACT II

SCENE 1

Cue 7	JACQUES: "... make me sick!" *Telephone rings*	(page 29)
Cue 8	ESME: "... consider us a bit." *A bell rings*	(page 32)
Cue 9	DELACHAUME: "Camomile tea ..." *A bell rings*	(page 32)

SCENE 2

No cues

ACT III

Cue 10	GEORGES: "... to live now." *A car door slams off*	(page 65)

www.ingramcontent.com/pod-product-compliance
Ingram Content Group UK Ltd.
Pitfield, Milton Keynes, MK11 3LW, UK
UKHW021846210426
5322IPUK00022B/494